Working with the
dreaming body

By the same author

Dreambody: The Body's Role
in Revealing the Self

Working with the dreaming body

Arnold Mindell

Routledge & Kegan Paul
London and New York

First published in 1985
by Routledge & Kegan Paul plc

11 New Fetter Lane, London EC4P 4EE

Published in the USA by
Routledge & Kegan Paul Inc.
in association with Methuen Inc.
29 West 35th Street, New York, NY10001

Set in 10 on 13 point Palatino
by Set Fair
and printed in Great Britain
by The Thetford Press Limited, Thetford, Norfolk

Reprinted in 1986

Library of Congress Cataloging in Publication Data

Mindell, Arnold, 1940–
Working with the dreaming body.
Bibliography: p..
Includes index.
1. Medicine, Psychosomatic. 2. Dreams. 3. Psychological manifestations of
general diseases. I. Title.
RC49.M524   1985   616.08   84–18097

British Library CIP data also available
ISBN 0–7102–0465–5 (pb)
ISBN 0–7102–0609–7 (c)

Contents

Contents

Introduction

Working with the Dreaming Body is a book meant for the layman as well as for the practising doctor and psychologist. It is a book about finding the meaning behind physical disease. The concept of this book was recommended to me by the Dutch publishers, Mr and Mrs J. L. van Hensbroek. They read my book *Dreambody* (Sigo Press, Boston, California, 1982; Routledge & Kegan Paul, London, 1984) and felt that I should write another book connecting dreams and body phenomena which would be based mainly upon case reports.

I hesitated about beginning this new book because I felt that a text based upon case reports and directed to the layman would not be scientifically accurate enough to be of use to the professional. I wondered how a book could be written in conversational form, yet have a lasting value. If it's too informal, is it sufficiently exact or conservative?

I soon had a dream which quieted my doubts. In this dream, C. G. Jung came to me and asked me to get up at a meeting of the Health Committee of the United Nations and speak about my discoveries. This dream convinced me to begin this book. The essence of the text was then created by conversations between Englien Scholtes of Lemniscast and myself. This book came out like the snap of the bow. Englien and I both followed our excitement and energy, she did minimal yet important editing on the text, and I am infinitely grateful to her as well as to Mr and Mrs van Hensbroek for their patience and help with this work. I also want to thank Barbara Croci for helping me with last chapter on dying, Nora

1

Mindell for aiding me in the chapter on dreambody communication and Julie Diamond for editorial assistance with the English edition of this work.

Today, 85 years after Freud's introductory discoveries, we are left with a very fragmented legacy called modern psychology. Body therapies are split off from dream therapies and dream therapy is normally done without reference to body feelings. Relationship difficulties are either dealt with analytically, behaviourally, or as part of a system. People are treated like machines which can be programmed. Psychotic people are still locked up behind bars. The dying and diseased are chopped up by medicine men as if the flesh had no soul in it. It seems as if psychology is now composed of bits and pieces, an unintegrated spectrum of many different colours which are poorly, if at all, connected to each other.

This book introduces a single theoretical framework which integrates the immense variety of human psychology. I call this framework of psychology 'process work' because it is based upon discovering the exact mode or channel in which the person is moving. My basic idea is to uncover this human process, and follow it, whether it is diagnosed to be psychotic, terminal, group orientated, diseased or normal. Process-oriented psychology is discussed theoretically in my book *Dreambody*, and *River's Way* (Routledge & Kegan Paul, to be published). The present work differs from *Dreambody* in several ways. In the following chapters I stress practical work, not theory. I expand past theories and demonstrate how to work with physically ill people as well as with dying patients relationship crises, severely psychotic people and ordinary dreamers with simple body problems. In my opinion, if you work with a wide spectrum of situations, rather than specialize in only dream or body work, relationship conflicts, psychiatry, medicine or children's psychology, then your appreciation of the complete nature of any one given individual is fuller and richer.

In this book I concentrate on the relationship between dreams and body problems because this is of central concern to the public. I show how dream and body work can be applied to people who are interested in psychology, as well as to people who are concerned about their body symptoms but who have no special interest in psychology. Today I realize that one can begin the individuation process with a big dream or a terrifying symptom. By focusing on illness, psychology learns to appreciate the ordinary 'man on the street', and is extended to touch the everyday reality of people.

I've discovered that the body's symptoms are not necessarily pathological, that is, they are not just sicknesses which must be healed, repressed or cured. Symptoms are potentially meaningful and purposeful conditions. They could be the beginning of fantastic phases of life, or they could bring one amazingly close to the center of existence. They can also be a trip into another world, as well as a royal road into the development of the personality.

I've discovered, as well, that body symptoms are mirrored in dreams and that the reverse is also true. All dreams talk about, one way or the other, body conditions. Moreover, there is one more surprising discovery. All of your physical gestures, all your communications to others, such as your tone of voice, your tempo while speaking, your facial expressions and the funny motions you make with your arms and shoulders while speaking, are all mirrored in your dreams. In other words, your physical diseases and your problems in communication, your relationship problems, all these can be found in your dreams.

In order to understand the full implication of these discoveries for your everyday life, I use about fifty case reports, and talk about communication theory, dream and body work, Jungian psychology and even a smattering of physics. Anyone without special training in psychology or physics will understand the following chapters because they are basically self-explanatory, readable case stories. These stories are taken from verbatim reports from sessions in my practice, training seminars, mental clinics and ordinary hospitals during my work with normal, psychotic, physically ill and dying people. The wide spectrum applications of dreambodywork demonstrates a difference between this work and other therapeutic methods which are preprogrammed applications of some particular school of thought. Dreambodywork cannot be predicted ahead of time since it is based upon the therapist's ability to discover and amplify the client's individual verbal responses, dream reports, body gestures and family situations. Such work is thus constantly changing and challenges the therapist's ability to continually observe himself and his client. Known therapies may appear in this work and completely new and undiscovered procedures may spontaneously appear, applicable for only that moment and situation.

CHAPTER 1

Flashes of insight

I have been brewing over the relationship between dream and body phenomenon for many years. Even as a child I wrote my dreams down. In spite of my long analytic training, doctorate work in psychology and graduate work in theoretical physics, I still couldn't grasp the connection between dreams and the body.

Then, twelve years ago, I got sick. I was completely at a loss, because I didn't know how to work with my physical illness as I did with my dreams. I tried going to a doctor with my headaches, aches and pains in my joints but my ailments and my pain coerced me to find out more about the body and to determine how it really works.

I read practically everything that had been written on the body. I especially read works on medicine and Western psychology that deal with the body – Reich and Gestalt therapy. When I had finished all my reading and listening to other therapists, I had the feeling that they were manipulating the body, programming it and telling the client how their body should be. But I wanted to find out what the body itself had to say. How would the body behave when left alone? I asked myself, 'Why am I sick? What have my fevers, my aches and pains got to do with me, if anything at all?' I also

5

turned to books on Eastern philosophy and medicine, yoga, acupuncture and Buddhism, but all to no avail. I still didn't know what my sickness was telling me, or what the personal significance of my disease was.

I decided to watch people's bodily reactions very closely and take notes on exactly what they did. I noticed, for example, how someone would react when he had eczema. He would start to scratch and by so doing, make it worse. When somebody had a headache, he would shake his head even more, or if it were a pain in the eye, he would press on it. If someone had a stiff neck – instead of trying to make it better – he'd try to make it worse by bending his neck backwards to feel the pain. I found it very interesting and confusing to notice people's reactions to pain. How could it be possible that people try to feel their pain more, although they say that they want a pill to ease the pain?

One day, while I was watching my son, I noticed that he was breaking open a scab on his leg and making it bleed, and I suddenly realized that the body itself is trying to make the pain worse. The body also, of course, has mechanisms to make itself better, but one of the main mechanisms that had not yet been taken into consideration is the mechanism to worsen the condition. Since trying to heal the body is not always very successful, I thought, why not take the body's own approach and *amplify* symptoms? I decided then to accept that possibility that the body was amplifying its own problems and making them worse. I wanted to test this out, but didn't tell anybody about my new 'discovery' at first, because it seemed like such an outrageous idea.

That insight, coupled with an experience with a dying patient, led me to the discovery that amplifying body symptoms is indeed crucial to the meaning of the disease. A patient with whom I was working then was dying of stomach cancer. He was lying in the hospital bed, groaning and moaning in pain. Have you ever seen somebody who is dying? It's really quite sad and terrifying. They flip quickly between trance states, ordinary consciousness and extreme pain. Once, when he was able to speak, he told me that the tumor in his stomach was unbearably painful. I had an idea that we should focus on his proprioception, that is, his experience of the pain, so I told him that since he'd already been operated on unsuccessfully, we might try something new. He agreed, and so I suggested that he try to make the pain even worse.

He said he knew exactly how he could do that and told me that the pain felt like something in his stomach trying to break out. If he helped it break out, he said, the pain worsened. He lay on his back and started to increase the pressure in his stomach. He pushed his stomach out and kept pushing and pressing and exaggerating the pain until he felt as if he were going to explode. Suddenly, at the height of his pain, he shouted out, 'Oh Arny, I just want to explode, I've never been able to really explode!' At that point he switched out of his body experience and began to talk to me. He told me that he needed to explode and asked if I would help him to do so. 'My problem', he said, 'is that I've never expressed myself sufficiently, and even when I do, it's never enough.'

This problem is an ordinary, psychological problem that appears in many cases, but with him it became somatized and was pressing him now, urgently expressing itself in the form of a tumor. That was the end of our physical work together. He lay back and felt much better. Though he had been given only a short time to live and had been on the verge of death, his condition improved and he was discharged from the hospital. I went to see him afterwards very often, and every time he 'exploded' with me. He'd make noises, cry, shout and scream, with absolutely no encouragement on my part. His problem was clear to him; his ever-present body experiences made him acutely aware of what it was he had to do. He lived for two or three years longer and then finally died after having learned to express himself better. What it was that helped him, I don't know, but I do know that the work relieved his painful symptoms and helped him to develop.

It was then, also, that I discovered the vital link between

dreams and body symptoms. Shortly before he had entered
the hospital, the patient dreamed that he had an incurable
disease and that the medicine for it was like a bomb. When I
asked him about the bomb, he made a very emotional sound
and cried like a bomb dropping in the air, 'it goes up in the air
and spins around sshhhsss . . . pfftpff.' At that moment, I
knew that his cancer was the bomb in the dream. It was his
lost expression trying to come out, and finding no way out, it
came out in his body as the cancer, and in his dream as the
bomb. His everyday experience of the bomb was his cancer,
his body was literally exploding with pent-up expression. In
this way, his pain became his own medicine, just like the
dream stated, curing his one-sided lack of expression.

In a flash I understood that there must be something like a
dreambody, an entity which is dream and body at once. In
this case, clearly, dreams were mirroring body experiences
and vice versa. I had already had a hunch about the existence
of a dreambody from other cases, but this was the first insight
that I had had.

To date, I have not come across one case in which a body
symptom's process was not reflected in a dream, and I have
seen many hundreds of physically ill people and many
thousands of dreams. The dreambody in the case we have
just seen manifested itself in various channels. By channels I
mean various modes of perception. For example, the dreambody appeared visually as the firecracker in his dream. It was
felt by him proprioceptively as his pain, pressing him to
explode. It appeared afterwards as his shouting, in a verbal or
auditory channel. The dreambody, then, is a multi-chan-
nelled information sender asking you to receive its message
in many ways and noticing how its information appears over
and over again in dreams and body symptoms.

The way I discovered the concept of the dreambody was
through what I call amplification. I amplified my client's
body, or proprioceptive experience and I amplified the
exploding process which was mirrored in his dream. Amplification has become a very useful tool for me, and it has very

wide and meaningful applications. The basic idea of amplification is to discover the channel in which a dream or body process is trying to manifest itself, and to amplify according to the channel. For instance, if a client tells me a dream about a snake and simultaneously he moves his hands to describe it, I might amplify the process by moving my arms or asking him to move his arms even more, or suggest that he move like a snake. If a client gave great detail as to the color, size and shape of the snake, I would note that the visual channel is important and I might amplify the process by asking him to see the snake more accurately and pay careful attention to his vision of the snake.

Amplification makes the term dreamwork theoretically no different than the term bodywork. Both dreams and body phenomena are simply pieces of information coming from the dreambody's visual and proprioceptive channels. Dream-bodywork does not even need the terms dream, body, matter or psyche, but instead, works with processes as they appear. This work is based upon the exact information according to its channels. The therapist's only tool is his ability to observe processes. He has no pre-established tricks or routines. This makes his work unpredictable and related only to that specific individual situation which is happening.

For me, process work is a natural science. A process-oriented psychologist studies and follows nature, while a therapist programmes what he thinks should be happening. I don't believe in therapy because I don't know any more what is right for other people. I have seen so many strange cases that I have decided to go back to my original idea as a scientist. I simply look to see what exactly is happening in the other person and what happens to me while he is reacting. I let the dreambody processes tell me what wants to happen and what to do next. That is the only pattern I follow. I do not press people. Their bodies and souls know better than I do. When people get healthy, I'm happy, but I no longer care about that so much any more. It is more important that things should take their natural course. Whatever happens, seems to be their fate, their Tao, their journey on earth – it looks as though it is their pattern to either worsen and die or to live a life of terrible pain.

In some cases it seems that the more you try to take the pain away, the worse it becomes. In these cases, also, I still amplify their pain and people feel better, living their diseases because their disease then becomes a meaningful experience that is constantly pressing them towards consciousness. It wakes them up. Many people, on the other hand, are looking for a cure and say they just want to be relieved of their symptoms. I tell them to go ahead if that's what they want – how should I know what's right for them? Go ahead and try whatever you like, go and take the magical medicine trip against disease and do what you need to, and if it works – fantastic. Very often, however, these therapies and cures don't work. It might be the person's fate to be living in the late twentieth century with an incurable disease.

At the time I began working with dying people, I could not figure out why sometimes I had miraculous effects and othertimes I failed miserably. Thank God, I had some background in theoretical physics, because my scientific nature helped me to understand my adventurous and often blundering ways, which produced as many radical effects as it did 'duds'. The first thing I said to myself was that I needed to work with the process, living, dying or whatever. I use the term process like a physicist, not like a psychologist. The psychologists, especially the Gestalt psychologists who have made the term process famous in psychology, do not define their term. They differentiate it from 'content', which is what people say. For me, process includes content. I see process in two forms, primary and secondary processes. Primary processes are closer to awareness, and include content, that is, that which you talk about. Secondary processes are all the unconscious phenomena, like body symptoms, of which you are only vaguely aware, and to which you have very little relationship, that is, which you cannot control.

I generally think of process work as a train. The train stops at various train stops, then moves on. Normally, people think in terms of the train stations, or in terms of 'states'. We say that someone is nuts, or sick, or dying, but these are just the names of the train stations. I'm interested in the flow of things, not the name of the tumor, but the way it develops, what it does and says to the person. The movement of the train fascinates me, and the movement of the train is what I call process. Another analogy I think of is a river. A river flows and flows and at the source it often looks very peaceful. But underneath, where we do not see, the deeper water, or secondary processes, flows over dragons and pits, empty abysses and scary whirlpools.

Process work saves me from judgments. If I think in terms of process, I cannot think in terms of good or bad, sick and healthy, past or future. If I think in terms of process, then I can work nonverbally, with comas or with meditation, and I don't get stuck with words. If I think of process then I look at the overall situation.

The different channels of the process are like the little streams which go off from the bigger river. If you do not know about channels, then you will work only physically, or only with the dreams of your client, and you'll miss the bends and turns in the river, which make all the difference in the world.

Communication concepts, like channels and process, are devoted towards the most basic elements, the most archetypal behavior of all human beings. By using the neutral language of process and channels, we can understand and work with people from all over the world, without even understanding the exact meaning of their words. We can now follow them through insane states, near-death conditions, and even through comas, when they're not tied down to the images and limiting concepts of our own culture, like mind and matter, psyche and soma.

Another interesting example of working with the dreambody of those near death comes to mind. A little girl came to see me with a rapidly growing tumor in her back. She was

11

dying and those around her were ready to say goodbye to her. She had already been operated on several times and her doctor told me that she was a very unhappy child. He said that I could play with her and work with her since all the others had given up hope. The little girl came in and told me that she had dreamt that she let go of the safety fences around a very dangerous lake. Then she lay down on the floor and told me that she wanted to fly. She had a corset on her back because the tumor had weakened her spine and she said she couldn't fly with it on. I was afraid to take it off. I phoned her doctor and promised that I would be very careful with her, but could I remove the corset from her back so that we could fly? He told me again that she was such an unhappy child and as nothing worse could happen to her any more, I could go ahead and remove the corset. We took it off and she lay on her stomach and started to make flying motions with her arms. She said she was flying.

'Oh, Doctor, I'm flying – it's such fun', she laughed. I amplified the flying movements of her arms and we 'flew' together. She squealed with delight and told me we were going over a cloud.

'Yes', I encouraged her, 'I'm underneath you and can see you way up there.' Then she told me it was my turn to go up there, and she'd watch me. We 'flew' like that for a while and then she said, 'Well, I'm not coming down anymore.'

'But why?' I asked.

'Because I want to fly around to all the other planets,' she answered. I got really scared and thought to myself that if she 'flew' away, she might die. Nevertheless, I wanted to see what her process really was. Maybe it was right for her to fly away – who was I to know? I told her that she must make the decision herself; whether she wanted to fly away to other planets, or to come down. But she told me she was going away to the other planets, 'I'm going away to another world' a beautiful world where there are strange planets,' she told me.

Then came the crisis moment, I told her to go ahead and do it if that's what she had to do. She started to 'fly' away.

12

Suddenly, she looked back at me and began to cry. She said she didn't want to go without me because we were the only ones who 'flew' together. We both cried then, and hugged each other.

'I'll come down for awhile just to be with you,' she said. I told her to do what she felt she needed to. She wanted to first come back to earth for awhile so that we could play some games together and then she'd go to the other planets when she was ready.

This little girl improved rapidly and soon she could take her corset off, and even the tumor disappeared. It was obviously her process to come back down to the earth for a while. More specifically, it was her process to 'fly'. That is, to play kinesthetically and be free to move about. Her process started out in a kinesthetic channel and moved into a visual one, when she was seeing the planets and clouds. Then, she ended in a proprioceptive channel, feeling the sadness of leaving this earth.

Another example of amplification and the dreambody is the story of a man who was suffering from multiple sclerosis, and although he knew the 'cause', he did not want to change his pattern of living and allow himself to get better.

Multiple sclerosis is a disease in which the spinal column slowly deteriorates and the limbs gradually weaken. This disease, like other diseases, is related to the individual's psychology. A chronic disease is often a lifelong problem, a part of someone's individuation process. I don't believe that a person actually creates disease, but that his soul is expressing an important message to him through the disease.

The man who had multiple sclerosis walked into my room on crutches. He was shaking back and forth.

'I notice that you are shaking back and forth', I told him, 'but shaking may be the right thing for you.'

'Who are you to say that it's right?' he retorted. I told him that the very fact that it was happening to him meant that it was right. After all, I pointed out, *he* wasn't doing it. This he agreed to. I apologized for even mentioning anything.

13

'Should we just drop the subject then?' I asked him. But he said he wanted to find out more and know what I meant by my cryptic statement. He suggested that we try to find out why. I asked him to put his crutches down. This is a terrifying experience for a man who cannot stand. When he put them down I told him to experience everything that was happening to him while he was standing there without support.

Again, he got very angry and refused my suggestion. So I reversed my approach, picked up his crutches, gave them back to him and said, 'Let's just forget it.' But still, he was very curious about his terrible disease and wanted to find out more about it. He decided to drop his crutches after all and began shaking back and forth like a drunk. He couldn't walk, his legs just wouldn't work. Suddenly, he fell.

'I feel as if something pulled me down,' he said to me. I ventured that he try the experiment again and while he was falling, to watch very carefully and see just what it was that was pulling him down. As he stood up again, he told me that it felt like someone else was controlling him; he was no longer in control of himself. Then he told me that although he had never had control over himself, he had always wanted to be his own master and in complete control. For example, he said, he had just 'fallen' in love and wanted to stop loving, but couldn't. Here, too, it seemed as though something else was making him fall.

I explained to him that while I did not blame him for wanting to control his life, this experience of no-control was his process and that he should continue with it. Then, he took courage and stood perfectly well – he even stopped shaking – like you or me, he stood completely normally. 'Wow, it's amazing,' he said, 'if I let go, I can stand perfectly still.'

'Naturally, but now will you let your love life go in the same way?' I asked.

In spite of the fact that he had just had this tremendous insight to his problem, he hesitated and admitted that he didn't think he could let go, he still wanted very much to be in control. I told him to go ahead and do what he had to do with his life, but every time he got nervous about his multiple sclerosis and how it was developing, he could identify with the disease process – not his ego – and let go, get himself to lose control. Here is quite a paradox. Diseases can be self-healing; the dreambody is its own solution. If he upsets his drive for control, he has more control! Taking a risk often turns out to be the safest measure.

This is a message we have seen before. The man with an exploding stomach, diagnosed as a stomach tumor, also had a self-healing process. Exploding is your medicine, his body said to him. The girl who dreamed of letting go of the safety railing had a process of letting go. Her tumor was getting her ready to leave this world. In the moment of her departure, she had the power to decide to return. Discover the process, amplify its channel, and a symptom can turn into a medicine.

CHAPTER 2

From illness to inner development

Many of the people I see are not the least bit interested in psychology. In fact, they suspect analysts of being slightly crazy themselves, and think clients are neurotic and sick people, and that no one should go to see an analyst unless he is absolutely nuts. Some of these people have the right idea. Not all psychologists are trustworthy, psychology is not yet a perfected science, and it does depend on teamwork in order to function properly.

Many of these so-called 'therapy-resistant' people are among your most average friends and neighbors. The most fascinating thing about them is that they begin to show interest in their inner life when they are troubled by diseases. The terminally ill become especially open to change. Like all people, the fear of death sends them to the doctor. This same fear provokes them, it stimulates their awareness and often sets them on the trip of consciousness. Today, there are an increasing number of doctors who want to know more about psychology. More physicians than ever before are aware that some of their patients suffer from problems which cannot be healed by a pill or the scalpel alone. In spite of their reasons for entering analysis, these people present the most interesting work for the dreambody psychologist, for they are the majority of the population which form the mainstay of our culture. But the question is, how do we work with them? It's a most difficult question, for they only show interest in being healed, and claim that they never dream.

Frau Herman is such a person. After telling me her story and the details of her medical history, she promptly took off her blouse so that I could examine the many lumps under her arm. The tumors there had been diagnosed as cancer. She had widely spread metastases in her chest, and this, her second occurrence of cancer, was diagnosed as inoperable. As she talked (non-stop) to me about her cancer, I noticed that she was swinging between hopefulness and fatalism, preparing for her death. There was no indication that she wanted anything but a pill. In the midst of our conversation, I realized that she was pressing me into the medical routine of writing up her case history. I don't like taking case histories, but as I couldn't do anything else with her, I decided to follow her process and comply with what she was asking for. Suddenly, one interesting and surprising fact arose.

Three months before the first outbreak of cancer, her mother died.

'She was a domineering and controlling person, trying to make everything perfect,' Frau Herman explained to me. And another interesting statement came out. She said, 'My tumors feel like hardening, toughening.' I noticed that this symptom came after the death of her mother. I had an idea. If her secondary process was to harden up after the mother's death, she must have been able to live this hardness earlier, by being very hard on her own mother. I asked Frau Herman if she was very tough on her mother while she was alive. Frau Herman said that she was. I thought, her own mother is dead now, how can she be tough now on her own, inner mother? I theorized to myself that what she had disliked in her mother was that controlling nature. Frau Herman was able to fight this nature, extravertedly, while her mother was alive. But now that her mother was dead, her body was toughening up

17

in an attempt to fight this same controlling nature in herself, her own controlling perfectionism.

So I asked her what she would do if she could let go of her controls, her perfectionisms. Immediately she answered with a smile, 'I'd go to the North Pole.'

'O.K.' I said, 'do it. Otherwise you'd be just like your mother.'

She was utterly shocked. At first she said she couldn't do something that outrageous; after all, her husband would never have the time. I pressed her, and reminded her that she might not be around that much longer, and it might even be good medicine for her to go. So she actually let go of her controls and went to the nearest travel bureau.

Frau Herman was overjoyed to be rid of her mother's control. Her mother's death became her advantage. Here, death actually may have saved her life! Her inner development, letting go of her perfectionism and her rigidity, came through her body. Her beginning development was minimal, it had to be oriented to her mind, body and life situation. Happily, she reported the next week to me that she wanted to live again. She had had a great dream (the first one in her life that she remembered) that she was now going to a gym class where she could learn to be more flexible. That was the psychological work of Frau Herman, her tumors helped her to harden up against her mother, which is her own, inner-controlling nature.

Frau Herman is one of the many therapy-resistant people I referred to earlier. They would never let go to see an ordinary psychologist because they maintain that it is only their physical bodies that are in pain and that their problem has nothing to do with their minds. They don't know about the connection between their illness and their psychological process.

Another such woman came to see me. She told me that her only problem was that there was too much milk in her breasts and she wanted to be rid of the excess milk. Her doctor had tried everything and failed; eventually he sent her to me saying, 'At least it won't make you ill if you go see him.' She entered my consultation room and immediately told me, 'I hate psychology. I don't know anything about my feelings, and I don't really care to. The only thing I'm interested in is my breasts. I want to get rid of this milk in them.'

Years ago I would not have regarded this woman as ready for psychology, but now I thought that she would be an interesting case. She interested me because she had a different outlook, a different 'religion' than I, and I thought that, since I'm interested in the mind and psychology, I might learn something from her. I suggested that we forget about psychology.

'Let's talk about your breasts,' I said. 'Do you like them?' 'Don't ask such stupid questions,' she replied sharply. 'My breasts are full, overflowing with milk and I want to be rid of that. I don't want to become involved in these psychological questions.'

I apologized to her and said that I hadn't really meant to talk about her breasts, but I was under the impression that they were her problem.

'No, they're not my problem. I don't have any psychological problems,' she told me.

'Oh, well, what shall we do then?' I offered.

'Well, one thing I can tell you is that I hate my husband. He's terrible. He never touches or caresses me, and he never has time to spend with me. I hate him,' she stated. I had a feeling that perhaps she was projecting something on to him. I asked her why she didn't tackle the problem with her husband and explain to him how she felt. I suggested that perhaps by talking to him, he would understand her problem and together they could improve their relationship.

'But I can't,' she explained. 'He's too stupid.'

Turning the position around, I suggested, 'I think that you are projecting a part of yourself on your husband. In fact, perhaps it is you who isn't very sensitive or caring.'

'What are you talking about? You're really very stupid for a psychologist,' she said, quite irritated with me by now.

19

Again, I apologized to her for being mistaken. Then she continued, 'One thing I can tell you about myself that you should know, is that I had a dream in which I was an abandoned child.' This was a clue. I told her that this dream showed that she should be more warm and loving towards herself, that she had, in fact, somehow been abandoning herself. That seemed to work. She asked, 'What exactly do you mean?' 'Spoil yourself a bit to begin with,' I said, that appealed to her immediately. She asked me how she could go about doing that. 'Well, be more mothering towards yourself,' I replied. I made a few suggestions; she could sleep a little later, give herself a present. I gave her many basic and uncomplicated ideas. 'Just don't be too hard on yourself,' I summed up.

As she was leaving my practice, she turned to me and said quite spontaneously, 'I know why I have too much milk, it's because I'm not drinking it, I ought to be mothering myself more.'

You see, this is how psychology came to this woman; it came through her body. Basically, she was a very intelligent woman. She had had a very hard life and had, in turn, become very hard on herself. She no longer had any natural feelings and as a result, her body produced milk to make her be a mother, to find the maternal instinct within herself and to soften up. She also had not menstruated in a long time. This could have been because she still needed to remain a child in order to learn how to mother herself. I sent her to a very mothering psychologist. She had a wonderful effect on her. This woman with the milk in her breasts is in some ways a typical medical case whose symptoms were trying to motivate her to completely change her personality.

Let's look at another example of a patient who hated psychology, dreams and body symptoms. She was dying of cancer, had several growths in the spinal column and a huge lump on her neck. She came to see me because her doctor had sent her on account of a death phobia. As she walked in, she warned me that she had already been to see a psychiatrist and had refused to pay him because he told her she was going to die. Instinctively, I felt like fighting with her because she was so aggressive. A good fight might have even done her good. However, she looked so weak that I decided to ignore her aggression, sit back, be quiet and control myself. So I merely said that he could have been mistaken. But she was a most irritating woman. After a few minutes with her I could understand completely how the psychiatrist was driven to tell her that she was going to die.

Partly to beat this woman at her own game, I decided to listen to her story. Why was she so angry? She told me that she had a terrible recurring nightmare, and if only I could rid her of this dream, then she would pay me. 'There is a gray woman coming out of the grave, fusing with me and then going back. Hell, this is the most terrifying vision, get rid of it, please, get rid of it,' she pleaded with me. I thought to myself that the gray figure was probably her double, or her eternal self, going into her body and then going out of her body after her 'death'. From this dream I assumed that it was her process to die, but her double's process to go on and transcend life. How could I tell her this, though? She hated the whole idea of death and wanted only to be rid of it.

'Yes, it's a terrible dream,' I agreed. 'Let's just forget it.'

She was enormously relieved, 'Oh, you're an intelligent doctor. At last I'm meeting someone with some sense, but I want to destroy this dream and enjoy my life. I also had a dream about my husband. He's a terrible creature and tries to stop me from enjoying life. I dreamt that I wanted to kill him. I almost did, but couldn't bring myself to actually do it. Doctor, how can I get rid of my husband, he's killing me?'

It seemed to me as if her husband was her own inhibitions which kept her from enjoying life and that 'he' was the object of her aggressions. Thus, I decided to strike out at what he symbolized. 'Why don't you just forget about dying and have a good time?' I proposed. She was most surprised at this idea and acted as though she couldn't understand why she hadn't thought of it herself.

'I don't think you're going to die now, anyhow,' I said. 'Why don't you go and have a good time. Go skiing.'

'How did you know that I like skiing? I just love it.' She paused for a while, then said, 'I should live as if I'm going to live hundreds of years.'

This was the paradoxical way she suddenly integrated dying and immortality. She was right. She now had the attitude of the double that she would have a good time and live as if she were going to live forever, as if she was immortal. The idea actually meant something to her. Of course, her physical body will die sometime but another part of her will live forever, just as she wanted to believe. She was not simply repressing her own death, but had realized unconsciously that she will go on after death. A couple of weeks later, she was walking quite well, determined to have a good time. She really was enjoying herself for the first time. She wrote to me and told me that I had freed her from her husband, her psychological husband which she said symbolized her own inhibited self. This woman, I feel, has an individuation process that goes beyond life and death.

Some people need to feel that they will live forever, while others must know that this is their last life, the last chance they've got. They need to know that they must become whole now, in this lifetime. Living with the idea that life exists only in the moment is the correct psychology for some people, if they dream or visualize that this life is the end. I tell these people that they should consider the possibility that their disease might be their end, that they will not come back for more growth and these last days on earth they should strive to become whole.

I have seen such terrible suffering in my work. I've rarely come across cases where people have beautiful endings, as many books describe. Most of the people I deal with are ordinary people who are dying unfortunate deaths. When you tell these people that they have to live right now, fantastic inner changes often happen.

I recall recently seeing a business man, lying in the

hospital, dying of cancer, only having a few days left to live. I saw him with his doctor. The dying man feebly said, 'I'm dying, but thank goodness there's another world to go to.' Then he asked me, 'Do you believe in another world?' I said, 'Yes, for me, but I wouldn't put my trip on you.' He became upset and asked if not everyone had their own heaven. I said that I didn't know, I listened to the individual. I asked him, 'Did you ever have a dream or body experience which said there's another world?' He said he hadn't. Then I said, 'Well, you must live now, as if there's no other world, unless you have such a dream or an overwhelming experience which convinces you of the other world.' You cannot imagine how angry his doctor got at me. 'Don't take away his belief system,' he yelled at me. I replied that I follow the patient's process, not the doctor's beliefs.

At this point, the patient rolled over and threw up. He said he was very upset. I told him that if he had stuff to do in this life, he should not hang around dying, but should get his business done. Then I left. His doctor told me that several hours later, after taking the tubes out of his arms and signing a paper relieving the hospital of responsibility, the man left his room, went downtown to his business office, cleaned up his business, went home to his wife, and put things in order there, too. The man rapidly improved, and then, suddenly, many months later, died a relatively happy death. He apparently needed to think that this world was finite, and he had no other chance to straighten out his life. Everyone is individual. Sometimes it's right for a person to go 'Californ- ian', and get into dying and far-out experiences, and other times it is right to be totally down to earth and to live as if this world is the end.

Another man, a chronically schizophrenic person, dreamed that this life was not the end, that, in fact, he would go on developing even after his death. He was locked up in a mental asylum and had acute, constant attacks of schizo- phrenia, he would become wild and see himself as God or Napoleon. He often tried to commit suicide and because of this the head of the institution sent him to me. 'I just want to die,' he told me straight away. Perhaps it was his process to die, but I first had to convince myself. I decided to experiment with his suicidal tendencies. I told him that I had some pills that would kill him if he took them. In fact, they were just aspirin, but he didn't know that. He was very eager to take them. I gave him the pills and watched him very closely for any double signals, looking for any part of his system which may not agree with his desire to kill himself. There was absolutely no trace of any disagreement – his whole mind and body were congruently wanting to die. His eyes, his face, his mouth, his body, were all in harmony with the idea of death. I watched his skin, the dilation of his eyes, the movements of his arms, his fingers, I listened closely to his breathing, his sounds. There was not the slightest indication anywhere of hesitation as he took those pills. He took all five of them. Then I admitted that they were only aspirins, but that I needed to see his whole reaction to give me the necessary information to help him.

He was very depressed at having been deceived, 'I haven't met an honest person anywhere,' he said.

I explained, 'I was not being honest with you because, as an analyst, I needed to know whether this dying was really your process. Whether you should die or not.'

'I don't care anyway,' he said.

I was thoroughly convinced that it was his process to die. It was just too painful for him to continue living. Then he told me of a dream he had had. He dreamt that he killed himself and in the other world he had discovered that he had made a mistake. That dreamwork is one of my failures because I interpreted the dream to him by telling him he should not die because he would realize his mistake if he died. I did not follow, intellectually, his process, which was to die and come back, having realized his mistake. Although I interpreted the dream incorrectly, I took the right action. His body process told me that he wanted to die and should die.

I called his psychiatrist and told him that I was convinced

that this man's process was to die. 'I don't want him to die,' I said. 'But I think that he ought to be allowed to do what he needs to do, and in this case, it's to die.' I told him of the patient's dream. At that time, I believe, I interpreted the dream incorrectly. I was not enough of a Buddhist then to see that he would, or could, develop after his death, yet I was aware enough to see that life was not his present trip.

I told him to take a vacation. He was very happy to be allowed at last to go home. As soon as he got home, he took a driving test, got a licence, bought a pistol and shot himself in the head. That was his end. Unconsciously he was saying, 'Yes, there is another world. This world where I live with Arny and the psychiatrists is not the only world.' What I should have told him was, 'Yes, there is another world. When you kill yourself you will realize that death is no solution to your pain and come back.' Unfortunately, I was not developed enough at the time to have told him that. Nevertheless, I noticed all the information radiating from this patient, and it was congruent. His dream and body processes were telling him it was too painful now to live and that he was going to die, but that he'd come back.

Not only do certain mannerisms and body symptoms give a clue to the person's process, but also the very structure of the body often gives some information. A friend of mine, a student with a very prominent jaw, one that protruded much farther than normal, attended a course conducted by a very well-known body therapist. The therapist told this student that he was too intense, that his jaw needed to relax more. He worked on the jaw muscles at the back of his chin, put his fingers inside his mouth and watched for sensations in the mouth. After about thirty minutes, the student's jaw went into a more 'relaxed' position, and the student felt generally more relaxed. The next morning, however, he awoke and had no energy, felt listless and had lost the determination to do anything. He started to feel very low and sank further and further into depression . . . His attitude gradually worsened until he became suicidal.

25

All the determination that had been in his jaw had been taken out of him. It's possible to change people's whole psychological outlook by changing their physical structure. Thus, it is dangerous to restructure people simply because the restructuring goes along with a physical ideal or some theory of health. The term 'normal' cannot be generalized. Each individual has his or her own norm. The student did not have any pain in his jaw. The therapist simply deicided that it was too 'intense', not normal to have such a prominent jaw and decided to change it. The student then came to see me for help. I wondered what the best treatment would be because it was not natural causes that had made him change his behavioral pattern like this. He had been physically changed, yet his mind had not made the corresponding adjustment. It was not his process to be physically changed, and his suicidal feelings seemed to result from this physical change.

We decided to ask the *I-Ching* what to do about his condition. We came up with Hexagram 41, which is called 'Biting Through'. It was an amazing coincidence. We could have cast 63 other hexagrams, but it had to be this particular hexagram. The hexagram says that a person needs a strong jaw to bite through the problems in life with determination. This was exactly what he was not doing sufficiently. He had to work through many external difficulties instead of avoiding them as he tended to. He needed more control, not less control and relaxation. At this time in his life, it was just wrong for him to have a too relaxed attitude toward life.

It was an incredible example from the *I-Ching*. Like the body and dreams, the *I-Ching* also deals with process. At another time it could be right for him to relax and loosen up, but he was still in a 'biting-through' process. Process is a matter of what the Chinese call Tao. Timing a change in the body is not up to the therapist, but rather up to the person's body indications. This man's jaw was protruding. It wasn't a pathological symptom, but showed that his unconscious, through a postural signal, was saying to be more determined. He was not aware of his body signal. He did not have an

understanding relationship with it. If such a lack of awareness of the body continues for a long time, the body tends to
amplify its signals, it gets violent and angry and produces
unique body postures and vicious diseases. Now, after this
bitter experience, the student has more awareness of his
body. Slowly the jaw is regulating itself and coming back to a
more 'normal' position. He is consciously listening more to
his body and showing more determination. The timing is
right for that, and because he's making an effort, the jaw can
naturally relax. He's consciously picking up the signal, the
body need not exaggerate it anymore.

Body language is like dream language. It gives you
indications that the conscious mind is not yet able to give.
Once the mind is able to function in harmony with the body
signals, the body automatically relaxes. If the body is tense,
there is reason. The tension is needed, and shouldn't be
arbitrarily relaxed. If you can find and integrate the processes
in apparently lethal symptoms, powerful dreams and strange
acts of fate, you normally feel better and you have more
energy, yet you will also find that the new behavior not only
widens your personality but often brings you to the limits of
what you can do. Thus, a body symptom, regardless of how
seemingly insignificant, can become the most difficult and
exciting challenge in your life! A terrifying symptom is
usually your greatest dream trying to come true.

CHAPTER 3

Illness and projection

In addition to illness, another great problem which bothers everyone is projection, though most people don't recognize projection as a problem. Projection is a normal, psychological phenomenon, as normal as getting ill. Without even knowing that you are developing projections, you begin to love or hate someone, or begin to project negative or positive material on to someone.

Projection is so powerful that someone's negative projection can make you ill. And vice versa, a positive projection can inflate you or make you feel better. Jung talked of projection as feeling irritated about someone else or getting into an affect about someone when thinking about them. As you know, people can project anything which they are not yet aware of in themselves on to someone else. We can project our own wisdom, our stupidity, our lack of feeling, our intolerance, our egoism, our brilliance, etc.

The strongest thing about projections is that they are very difficult to withdraw. Many projections with a negative quality last for years and years, even among psychologists, whose profession it is to discover these projections and to integrate them back into themselves. It is almost impossible to see the projection in yourself.

Some projections can be withdrawn with a lot of work, but very often it is necessary to live them out, to really get into a fight with the person upon which you project something. However, as you can imagine, the fight usually ends much better if you are able to see the opponent in yourself. Nevertheless, if you are in a life and death struggle, or if you are a victim of war, we have to deal with the outer reality, and speak of projection only secondarily.

One of the reasons why projections are so difficult to integrate is because they are often tied up with body life. This discovery makes absolute sense if you stop and remember that dreams are mirror images of what happens in the body, and projections are also found in dreams. Therefore, projections are often intermingled with getting sick.

Think of someone you do not like. He is probably dangerous to you in some way, otherwise you would not get so upset about him. He does not love you, support you, or he is too controlling, evil, negative, etc. This negative person, or better said the negative projection, normally turns out to be the negative way in which you are dealing with some aspect of yourself.

Shamans and medicine men have unconsciously known this since the beginning of time. That is why all over the world, in China, India, Africa, South America and Alaska the most widespread and prevailing theory of illness is that you get sick because one of your enemies is conducting black magic against you. Today, thanks to the efforts of modern psychology, we know that our enemies can be very harmful, but we also know that they exist within us as well.

The way illness is directly related to these negative inner figures can be seen in the following case. A man came to see me with a very large goitre, which is a throat tumor around the thyroid gland. This man had an absolutely terrible projection upon his father. Despite spending years in analysis with different therapists, he still had wild affects against the old man. He found him to be a cold, dogmatic and hard man. His father, he felt, wanted to control everything.

But my patient told me that he did not come to see me because of his father problem, but because his large tumor was frightening him, and he was very scared about surgery. He showed me the immense goitre on his throat.

'Well,' I asked, 'how does it feel?'

'Oh, I don't feel any pain there,' he said, 'I don't think much about my body. In fact, to be quite honest with you, I don't feel bodywork is the thing for me. It is foreign to me and makes me nervous.'

I agreed, 'Okay we'll do what you want to do.'

'But I don't know what I want to do, all I know is that I am desperate. Please can you help me? I have been talking about my damned father for about ten years in analysis, and I am not interested in continuing to talk about him. I know all about him and still hate him!' With that last sentence, he slapped his hand hard on his knee.

'I hate him!' Again, he banged his hand on his knee and shouted, 'Arny, I just absolutely hate him, hate him, hate him!' He kept banging his poor knee. I have plenty of equipment for just this kind of reaction and immediately thought the punching bag would be a good idea for him.

'OK, here's my punching bag,' I told him. 'What do you mean, "here's my punching bag"?' he asked.

'Well,' I suggested, 'go ahead, hate your father, hate him some more, go on and really punch him hard, do what you're doing, but with more awareness.' He went to the punching bag and banged and banged while shouting, 'I hate you, I hate you.' There was no end to it. He punched a hole in the punching bag, put his hand right through it and kept going. He yelled so loudly that after ten minutes he went hoarse. Even still, he continued, although now only in a whisper, 'I hate you, I hate you.' His breathing was deep and rasping and his whole body was shaking with his hatred. Eventually, I asked him if he would like to stop because his voice was nearly finished.

'No,' he whispered. He cried and croaked and shouted on until he arrived at an insight. He suddenly sat quietly on my floor and said, 'Oh my God, it's been my father who has stopped me from shouting and punching!' What happened in this case? This man's father was controlling, hard and patriarchal. The father, the inner father was in control. That is, my patient was too controlling with himself. His father was a symbol of the way he dealt with his own problems. He spent too much time thinking, analysing and talking about his father problem, and by so doing was like the controlling father himself. He was controlling his basic process, which was anger, shouting and punching. In other words, he was working on his father complex as his father would!

When this man first came to see me, his voice was very quiet and timid. He had no energy and looked ill and depressed. All his energy was tied up by his father, so to speak, in his throat. By yelling and screaming, he let the anger and meanness in himself out, and he killed two birds with one stone. He was able to let his process proceed in the right direction, and he was able to relieve the energy in his throat. He had to realize that his father is the one in him who is controlling, but, paradoxically, the only way he could realize this was by learning in the body what it meant to let go of control.

It is interesting to me that this man's throat problem also makes him more aware of his voice, his throat center of consciousness. Just as the mind has its individuation process insofar as one learns about the different parts of oneself, so the body, too, wants to individuate and discover all of its potentials. The body has many centers and points of awareness. Your body uses projections and psychological problems to stimulate discovery of its different parts. Stomach problems raise consciousness of the stomach area, neck difficulties bring your relationship between the head and the body into awareness, and heart problems can frequently make you more aware of your feelings.

A basic psychological characteristic, like a negative father or mother complex, slowly transforms over the years as it uses different body centers. One phase of your life teaches

31

you about your legs, then you might spend years working on your back, seemingly with the same psychological complex. Likewise, a chronic body problem may be tied up with various psychological problems so that one season your mother complex can be found in your stomach, while in the next, your father appears there. This variation of psychological images connected to one or more body centers makes one-dimensional, psychosomatic studies which try to find out if behavior creates symptoms appear useless. All that we can say for the moment is that if you really get to the root of a process, then your projections can be integrated and the experience of the disease changes radically.

If you think that process work can heal you, we come up against a thorny problem. You will remember from the last chapter that I talked about process in contrast to states. Healing and disease are train stops on the train line. You can get off at these stops, or you can get back on the train. But for me, and for your life energy, healing and sickness are merely states. If you do process work, you are interested in the total life process and this means you are not interested in just one train station. You want to go the whole line. Your process can bring you everything you need in time. If you learn to follow your process without aiming at one station, or goal, then you become an individuated person. Your life becomes richer and you learn to reduce your projections, and integrate your pain.

Another interesting note for us to make at this point is that projection is itself a process. It does no good merely to say that you have a negative father complex. That's merely the train stop. You are better off if you can get on the train, go into your affect, and then at a later date, you can get off at the station called Insight. You first may have to start out hating the father, and then you may end up being a bit like him, capable of analysing everything coolly and intellectually. Process will take you from affect to insight. But if you try to reach the station called Insight before you pass through the town called Emotion, you never reach your destination. The man we were just working with tried to reach insight before going through a necessary and physical affect, and for ten years didn't get anywhere with his problems. In practice, I see people at all possible points between affect and insight. Some get stuck on the affect, while others stay too long at insight. Few take the trip wherever it goes.

The biggest problem I encounter is that people have not learned how to work with their feelings. One in a million mothers or fathers say to their children, 'Tell me, how are you feeling in your stomach, in your legs, in your joints? Tell me about your headache.' On the contrary, our whole culture is against feeling too much pain. People have still not learned to love themselves, and they have to learn it, they must make a different relationship with themselves towards their bodies. There is no way around it. It's important to accept pain, to sit with it and feel it. Many negative projections stem from channel blocks, from an unconsciousness of feeling and proprioceptive life. A positive projection on someone can be just as dangerous as a negative projection. All of your body experience is still projected outside yourself. This means that you are still not a positive lover towards yourself. In fact, a positive projection is even more difficult to integrate than a negative one because it is so pleasant. But for you there is something impoverishing in it, therefore, psychologically speaking, it is just as dangerous.

This lack of relationship towards their own bodies makes people very reluctant and shy about bodywork. I once had a patient who was dying from cancer and was in agony. He had tumors all over his body, but didn't talk about it. I came to his hospital room and the only thing he wanted to talk about was his wife.

'My wife, Arny, my wife,' he complained. 'She is so cold, she never kisses me, she never holds my hand and she's always tired. She's a decent and intelligent woman, but not at all a sweet woman.'

I happened to know this woman and it was not quite true what her husband said about her. I knew that she could be a sweet and caring woman. I thought that it was their relationship that was the problem. The main point was that this was the way that he felt, even if it were not true. It was important for me to see what he projected on to her and how he dealt with it.

'What shall I do?' he asked me. We had just had an extensive talk on bodywork so I said, 'Why don't you be more caring toward yourself? If your wife is not caring enough, then why not at least care more about yourself?'

'But what shall I do?' he asked in surprise.

'As I said, be more caring towards yourself. I don't have any prescriptions for that. Everybody is an individual.'

But he persisted, 'What does it mean to be more caring towards yourself?'

'Well, what do you want from your wife?' I asked.

'I'd like her to put her arm around my shoulder and her head on my chest,' he answered.

'O.K., go ahead and give me every detail.'

'Funny,' he said, entering into his vision, 'her head is on my chest and her arm is around my shoulder and yet I'm not thinking about sex. I'm just listening to her breathing.'

'Then let's listen to your breathing together, shall we?' I asked.

He was very reluctant. He was a 65-year-old Swiss gentleman, and listening to his breathing was as awkward for him as wearing a tuxedo is for a 17-year-old hippie. But he knew that he would die soon and dying people are always inclined to try something new. We listened to his breathing and then I asked him to amplify it. He made deep, loud noises for about twenty minutes. This deep breathing made him hyperventilate and after a while he laughed and said, 'Oh, why didn't I do this before. I feel drunk . . . I don't know what has happened to my pain.'

'What pain?' I asked in astonishment.

'All my tumors . . . all that pain has gone . . .' he said. He continued breathing for another twenty-five minutes while I amplified his body movements.

'Watch your shoulders while you're sitting, watch the

rhythm of your shoulders,' I said.

Then he said, 'I've just had the most fantastic vision. I'm going out into space and it's beautiful there. What am I going to do next?' When you work with your body, you heighten your proprioceptive or body awareness. By continuing this for about fifteen minutes, you often change channels from proprioception to vision and begin to fantasize. A vision is a surprising fantasy which moves you emotionally and physically. It is a picture of a physical experience. Likewise, if you discipline yourself to meditate upon a dream or a picture, after a while, you may feel it in your body.

After this vision, the patient fell asleep and dreamt that he was sitting in a circle. In this circle there was a man for every woman. Woman, man, woman, man were sitting together. The man and the woman opposite should make love together, but my patient saw between his penis and the woman's vagina a piece of wood which he had to remove. That was the end of the dream. I asked him what he associated to wood. He replied, 'Wood, blockhead, stupid.' He realized then how stupid he had been in his attitude towards his own body. Therefore, bringing up body problems and making him more aware of his body also brought him into contact with what Jung called the anima, the woman inside the man. She symbolizes his own feeling life and his ability to notice and to feel himself physically. We did more bodywork together and he came closer to his body, and therefore, his wife. Their relationship improved a great deal. He used his tumors to develop and to become much more sensitive and caring towards himself. The end of his life was rich and, according to one of his dreams, he died as an individuated man.

Bodywork which is successful depends totally on the patient. There are people who are kinesthetic types. They are inclined to act things out (like the man and the punching bag), they have processes which express themselves in physical movement, outwardly, extrovertedly and dramatically. For other people, such actions may be totally wrong and if you ask them to do it you can even make them sick. This patient with the tumors on his body was very introverted, he didn't express many of his feelings to me. I sat with him for forty minutes just breathing together with him, watching him. I could see that this was the right process for him, just feeling inwardly. The man with the goitre, however, needed to express himself far more violently and outwardly. Many therapists believe that you should dramatize everything and act everything out, but, as we've just seen, this isn't correct, because it depends on the individual's process.

Projections are psychosomatic phenomena which require both psychological insight and somatic consciousness to be worked through, withdrawn and integrated. They demand awareness of proprioception, as well as kinesthesia, and can't be withdrawn until the unknown or unused channels of awareness are developed.

CHAPTER 4

Switching channels

At the core of dreambodywork lie the fascinating phenomena which I call channel switching. Processes can switch
suddenly from hearing to feeling, from feeling to visualization, or from seeing to moving, like lightning. If you can
follow processes as they move in and out of the body, you are
then able to move with the flow of life, and sometimes
witness surprising things. For example, a man who came to
me had a strange habit of bending backwards. He bent so far
backwards, that I thought I should encourage him to bend
even further and see if I could get a clue as to why it was
necessary for him to bend. He bent backwards and then
started bending back the other way, i.e. forwards. He told me
that he had a tremendous amount of tension in his back. I put
my hand on his back as he was leaning forwards and asked
him what he wanted me to do next. He asked me to rub his
back and continue up and down his spine. Suddenly I
touched a lumpy knot. I pushed it a little harder and he cried
out in pain. I thought it was better not to push so hard but he
asked me to do it again and to continue doing it. The pain in
his back increased as I pushed, but he begged me to carry on.
People have a huge need to feel their pain. Very often pain is
the beginning of a great deal of awareness. As an energy

center, it awakens consciousness. I continued pressing, and the pain became so intense that he suddenly shouted, 'I see it!' He automatically switched channels.

Initially, this man was moving his back, then he was proprioceping his pain. By moving his body and bending it, he suddenly switched channels and a picture appeared. That is important. When situations become too extreme or painful in one perception channel, when they reach their limit or edge, the experience switches suddenly and automatically from one channel to the other. I had worked with this man for about six months but had never experienced this switch with him before.

My finger was still in his back, I held it for a while and then let go.

'I see it,' he cried again, 'I see it!'

'Tell me what you are seeing,' I asked.

'I see somebody standing behind me poking his finger in my back.'

'Why is he poking you in the back?' I wanted to know.

'He's telling me that I should be more honest. I'm not being honest, I'm not showing all that's inside of me. I really hate to because I'm so shy. This finger is telling me I just have to be more honest.'

I put my finger in his back again and amplified it, 'Be more honest, do it!' I said. Then out poured all the stories that he had kept in and had not wanted to tell me before.

By my own sense of proprioception, that is, by touching him sensitively, I discovered something in another person and that discovery was the clue for him to be able to tell many problems that he had been storing up inside himself. His channel switched from the proprioceptive to the visual and unlocked the door that had been bolted for so long.

This switching from one channel to another is, to me, one of the most interesting aspects of dreambodywork. At a certain point, when you cannot stand the pain, a snap occurs. This happens in both mental and physical channels. When a person faints, it is because he cannot stand the pain of some experience any longer, so the channels switch. It is often at this point that the person has a dream or a vision which holds the key to his process. My definition of a vision is a powerful, shocking experience in the visual channel. A powerful body experience usually accompanies a vision. However, when you visualize your pain, the pain disappears. In this man's case both his pain and the knots in his spine disappeared. He succeeded in integrating what his knots were trying to show him. He became more honest and was able to understand his body experience.

What part of the individual is creating these knots and visions? I think that it's the absolute real personality, what I call the dreambody. The dreambody is a term for the total, multi-channeled personality. It expresses itself in any one or all of the possible channels I mentioned. It can also use the telepathic channel and can manifest itself in dreams. If you amplify a dream symbol, the process that results is the real you, the one you were before you were born and the one that you'll be after you die. The same result occurs when you amplify a body symptom. The eternal and total personality is exposed. The dreambody is the empirical name for a mystery which appears in practice as dreams and body life. With the discovery of the dreambody, dreamwork and bodywork have become interchangeable. I find that if I start working on the dream, it invariably switches to the body problem and vice versa. The dreambody is the part of you that is trying to grow and develop in this life. The dreambody is your wise signaller, giving you messages in many different dimensions. When it signals to you in the body, we call it a symptom. When it signals to you through a dream, we call it a symbol.

I can show you this best through a story of my own experience of changing channels. One night, I awoke in pain in the middle of the night and found that my left arm was partially paralyzed. I couldn't lift it. This is called neuritis and is an extremely painful condition. I decided to work on it with the help of some students from my training program in Zürich. I started to amplify the pain. I put my hand back and

39

almost fainted from the excruciating pain, but as I was about to faint, I switched channels from proprioception to visualization. I saw an old American Indian standing behind me. At the exact point in my back where the terrible pain was, he had put his hands. I switched into the acoustic channel and heard him say to me, 'You've got to change!'

I asked him in desperation how I could do that.

He replied, 'You're now in your mid-forties, you've got to change, I no longer want you to identify yourself as a human being.'

I became furious, 'But I'm just a normal human being with a family and large practice, get out of here.'

'No, you now have to identify yourself as a spirit,' he demanded.

'Are you out of your mind? I'm not a spirit. I'm just an ordinary guy who pays taxes.' I insisted.

'All right, if you continue talking to me like that, I'll kill you!' he told me.

That shook me up and had me convinced, so I agreed to take a look at his world, to try and identify more with him, this old Indian. I saw that I had been complying with other people's ideas of what and who I was and what I should be doing, so I decided to give up my personal history and be more of an individual. Even though I'm not a very conventional person, this Indian was telling me I should be even more of my unique self. Afterwards, I went home and fell asleep. The pain improved and I dreamt that I was walking down a path. There was something behind me . . . I turned slowly around and there he was, as big as a tree . . . my double. He was thousands of years old and was trying to tell me that I should identify with my real age, my hundred-thousand-year-old personality. At this time this wasn't easy to accept, but as the signal was so strong, I thought I should at least try. I wondered now whether I should take this neuritis, the body symptom, and be totally responsible for it myself, or work on it with a physician. I decided to stay with the pain and take the responsibility for the Indian and let it change me. Everytime the pain began to get unbearable, I switched to my double and talked to him.

This intense pain, switching it off and being able to see my double, continued for a whole month. While my arm was improving, I changed radically. My double enabled me to be mediumistic, he could see into people's pasts and tell me everything about them. He was about 80 percent correct. This double is still awake, sometimes I lose awareness, but my double is often there. He speaks to me and I feel his presence. I still make lots of stupid mistakes like everybody else, but at other times I can be very aware. Sometimes I have this feeling of being the old personality, independent of culture, convention and time. This is an experience of my own dreambody. Now he's no longer just a vision, he has become part of my total body experience.

One woman's dreambodywork began with a dream, rather than with a body symptom. She is a very shy and practical woman and at the time was having difficulty in relationships, she found it hard to express her feelings. She had dreamed that she was with me and we went into a clinic. There was another patient of mine in this clinic with whom I worked. During our session, I asked this woman what she associated with this patient in the clinic, and she told me that this woman killed cats. I wondered how she would expect me to work with a woman who killed cats, and she said that I would probably tell her to be a cat and to make a game of it. I suggested that we work with this woman in the dream and that she should be a cat.

'Well, I don't quite know how to do that,' she hesitated.

'But what does a cat do?' I wanted to know.

'Miaow, miaow.' Suddenly she switched channels and to my surprise she was down on all fours and was doing, quite unconsciously, the Yoga cat posture. She made a very high arched back, and sighed very deeply, dropping her back down again. Then she started to stick her tongue out like a cat.

'Ooohh, I have the most terrible pain in my back!' she cried.

41

'What's wrong with your back?'

She then remembered that about eight years ago she had had a terrible pain in her lower back. Although she had vaguely mentioned this to me before, it did not have much significance then, because it was an unrelated piece of information. But now her body was working with it. I never tell people how and when to work with symptoms, I only encourage it if they really want to, and if their bodies give the signal.

'Oh my goodness, I have this terrible backache and it's related to the cat,' she discovered. 'When I do this posture, I feel better.'

This is an interesting case of bodywork resulting from a dream. If I had interpreted that dream, I would have said, 'My dear, you need to be a bit more of a cat in your relationships. That means, develop some claws and every now and then hiss to the people around you, and spit a little like a cat. Go ahead, pet with them, be sweet, but be a cat as well, be a cat now with me.'

I would never have thought of working on her back, but through the dreamwork her body problem came up. Now I can say to her that she should be a cat. She realizes by herself that being a cat doesn't mean just saying 'miaow', or being more feminine, but to learn to be more like a cat by using her entire body and by being more feisty and less compliant in her relationships. This is also an example of how Yoga can come up in dreambodywork, not as a technique, but arising naturally from an individual process.

With dreambodywork, you never really know what's going to happen. There's no program to follow, no therapeutic tricks or methods, just the awareness of the therapist. When I follow people's individual body processes, I come across every type of bodywork that's ever existed and some that I've never seen before. Sometimes, I even get results that I've never encountered before.

Recently, I was working with an advanced class of students. One of the students had a severe pain in her back, but didn't know what it was or how to deal with it. She thought it was possibly a nervous agitation. She had a dream in which she awoke in the middle of the night with a terrible shock. We started to work on her pain. She told me that she felt as if someone had put a tremendous amount of pressure on her back. One of the other students then went behind her and started pushing on her back and amplifying her experience of the backache. That afternoon we were working in a cabin in the mountains, and while he was pushing on her back, there was a sudden bang from the road nearby. It was a car accident. One car had backed up and crashed into the front of another. At least, that's what we initially thought. We saw the people get out of their cars and have a heated argument which disturbed our peace and concentration. We could hear them yelling at each other.

The student who was working was especially disturbed by the accident. When I asked her why it should disturb her so much and why it should have happened right then, she thought it could have been a synchronicity.

'Well,' I replied, 'I don't know if it was a synchronicity, but what do you experience right now? Your focus has changed. First you were focusing on your back and now there is a channel switch and you're focusing on the street. What do you experience?'

'Well,' she answered, 'I saw that woman in the front back her car into the car behind her. It was not he who was pushing her but she who backed into him. That makes a big difference.'

'What does it have to do with what we are doing here, then?' I wanted to know.

'We're doing it wrongly,' she said. 'I should be backing into the man behind me, he shouldn't be pushing me!' We tried it that way and she started pushing into the student behind her. They switched around and she was at the back. He pushed backwards into her and suddenly she shouted, 'Don't push, don't back into me. Stop it, you're trying to make trouble for me, if you don't cut it out, I'll kill you!'

43

At that point I asked her why she wanted to kill herself. The one at the back, who spoke those words said, 'Stop or I shall kill you and I am God . . . I insist that *you* stop pushing *me*. Let life be and let things happen. Let go and relax. Stop trying to push me around. You are the one who is making the trouble. I'm forced to resist you and that's why you are getting this pain in your back.'

The woman said that God was telling her to relax and let go and I told her to do so. She reacted by lying on the ground and breathing very deeply as in Yogic (Pranayama) breathing. Then she began to cry, her eyes still closed. I did not talk to her, but amplified her body motion by putting my hand on her chest and pushing it lightly. I was trying to amplify her feelings in accordance with the rhythm of her breath, almost like artificial respiration. After a while, she stopped breathing with long pauses, and tears started running down her cheeks.

Then she said, 'My goodness, I feel as though I'm with God, I feel as though I am God.' I said, 'Go ahead and be with Him.' She then had a tremendous, drug-like, religious experience (without the use of any drugs). She told me afterward that in a dream she had, she had been given a beautiful stone that she associated with God. Now she was given this wonderful experience. It was like a dream trying to happen. While coming out of this experience, she said, 'Y'know, I've lived my life wrong. I always tried to push my life and could never believe that life was right the way it was. Now, when I let go, I really feel I am with God.'

This was a genuine spiritual experience. As she was coming out of the experience, her eyes were crossed and she couldn't see straight. This is a typical sign of a person who has had a very deep experience. Actually, your eyes normally see two images and it's your mind that pushes the two images together and makes you see only one image. However, when you get deep into your body and you enter proprioception, you leave visual organization behind and realize again that your eyes are actually functioning separ-

44

ately and are not as important as you thought.

This student's backache, dream symbol and automobile accident were different channels, different perceptions of her dreambody. Her dreambody in this case was her God telling her to let Him be, not to push backwards against fate but go with it and live humbly. This example indicates that the dreambody is symmetrical; it is like a many-faceted jewel, a diamond, since all its sides, i.e. each of its channels, the world, dream, and body, reflect the same information in different ways. The dreambody is a diamond body and each of us is potentially a symmetrical jewel. Becoming yourself can be understood as knowing your dreambody, becoming whole or round, developing your full experience through awareness of each of your different channels.

In this last case, a process-oriented worker will be especially fascinated by the fact that the woman's process switched from her backache or proprioception, to an outer event, then back to her proprioception, and finally to a visualization and religious experience which was multi-channeled. It is important to be able to notice these channel switches in the work because the dreambody seems to want one to develop awareness of the various channels. The dreambody signals in one channel and then switches channels because it realizes that you have either come to the limits of what you can bear in one channel or else that you are on the wrong track and need to perceive things in a totally new light.

Switching channels can be a pretty mysterious thing. The switch from a body process to an occurrence in the world indicates that this woman's dreambody was in her back and in her environment as well. On the other hand, switching channels can also be a mundane thing which happens every day. A young person I know is trying to finish his exams. Often while he is concentrating and studying, a channel switch occurs. He's using his visual channel on his reading and remembering and finds that he often has to leave the library and go to the bathroom and masturbate. There, he visualizes a lovely young girl. Recently, I told him to go more into the body fantasy, and he reported that he talked to the girl and she told him to relax, to help her because she was so nervous. He did, and went to the movies instead of the library that day.

The opposite can happen as well. A woman or man about to make love may suddenly experience a loss of proprioception, that is, a temporary or permanent impotency which drowns orgasm. In practically all of these cases, there is no organic reason. There is simply a channel switch which the couple are not making, between proprioception and simple talking. Normally, there is a lot which one has missed consciously, a lot of problems which have not been worked out and which have not been talked about and which turn the body off.

But switching channels can also be a matter of life and death, it can even be the turning point of a severe illness. Recently, for example, a woman came to see me and she was very sick. Even while waiting in the waiting room, she was throwing up in the toilet. She had a high fever that day and severe stomach cramps which had been bothering her for about two weeks, as well as a heavy bronchitis. She had just come from her doctor who could not make a clear diagnosis about her stomach trouble or her fever.

She came in, looking down at the floor. I told her to follow the downward movement of her need and let her body do what it wanted. She immediately lay down on the floor and began to roll around. At one point she rolled over on to me as I was now sitting on my floor, too. With her back against my chest, she began to murmur that she felt very, very sick. She said, slowly but repetitively, that she had a burning sensation in her stomach. I recommended that she put her total focus on her stomach and internally amplify her proprioception. 'Make your stomach burn a bit more,' I said.

She did and said that it burned like a fire. Then she told me that it was bright and fiery with some orange and red in it. After she repeated this information to me a couple of times, I realized she was trying to change channels. This was a relief because her proprioception was so chaotic that it seemed as if her disease was running off with her without reserve in a channel in which she had little awareness. At once I said, 'See the colors, do not feel them anymore. Don't allow any feeling, only seeing.'

At this point, she was still moving her arms about in the air to describe (kinesthetically) her severe burning sensation. I told her to stop the movement and feeling and to switch to the colors which were appearing. After a minute or two she switched, and a very intense vision appeared. She lay across my back, motionless and saw the flames. In the fire, a man was coming to birth with a fire aura about him. After a while, he came forward and bowed in front of a goddess and received information about his life, information that he absolutely needed. I'm hesitant to go into the specific information, because what happened was meant for her, a matter of this woman's own personal myth.

I want to stress here the process of her disease. She was not sick. Her dreambody was appearing to her, it wanted her full attention, it wanted her out of work. It then wanted to switch out of proprioception and into a vision in order to inform her about her personal myth, her road in life and the meaning of her existence. To do this, her dreambody used colorful paints, so to speak, as well as powerful feelings.

If you are quick enough to observe a channel switch, flexible enough to work with visualization, proprioception, audition, kinesthesis and with parapsychological events happening on the street which grab your attention, then you'll be able to follow your own and other people's process, and be aware of which direction you are headed in in this life.

CHAPTER 5

Dreambody
in a fairy tale

The appearance of the dreambody depends upon the channel in which its process appears. Thus, it may occur as a pain, as a movement, or as voices in the ear. It can also appear on the city street, as a shocking event in the world, or it can appear visually in dreams. When a certain dream motif fits a small group of people we speak of a local saga. When the motif fits a culture, we speak of a fairy tale. Fairy tales are something like cultural dreams. As you read the following tale, try to guess what sort of people and what type of culture would be dreaming this kind of story.

There was once a poor woodcutter who worked from early morning till late at night. When he had finally saved a little money, he said to his son, 'You're my only child. I've made a little money by the sweat of my brow, and I'm going to spend it on your education. If you learn some decent trade, you'll be able to keep me in my old age, when my limbs are stiff and I must sit at home.' The boy went away to the university and studied hard. The teachers praised him and he stayed for a while. When he had almost completed his courses, his father's meager savings were finished and he had to return home. 'It's a shame,' said his father sadly. 'I have no more to give you, and in these hard times I can barely earn what's needed for our daily bread.' 'Dear father,' said the son, 'don't worry, I'll get used to this life and maybe I'll be the better for it in the end.'

As the father was preparing to go out and earn more money cutting and piling firewood, the son said, 'I'll come along and help you.' 'I don't know,' said the father. 'It might be hard on you, you're not used to heavy work. I doubt if you could stand it. Besides, I have only one axe and no money to buy another.' 'Go and ask our neighbour,' said the son, 'he'll let you have an axe until I've earned enough to buy one.'

The father borrowed an axe from the neighbour, and the next morning they went to the forest together. The young fellow helped his father and was as cheerful as could be. When the sun was high in the sky, the father said, 'Let's rest a while now and have something to eat.' The son took his bread and said, 'You rest father, I'm not tired. I'm going to take a little walk.' 'Don't be a fool,' said the father. 'What's the good of running around? Afterwards, you will be too tired to move. Stay here and sit down.'

But the son went deeper into the forest and ate his bread. He felt light and gay and looked up into the green branches, to see if he could find a nest. Back and forth he walked and at last came to a big angry looking oak tree, that must have been hundreds of years old and was so thick that five men couldn't have girdled it with their arms. He stopped, looked at the tree and thought, 'Lots of birds must have built their nests in that tree.' Suddenly, he heard someone calling. A muffled voice was crying, 'Let me out, let me out!' When he looked around, he couldn't see anything, but he thought that the voice came out of the ground.

'Where are you?' he cried.

The voice answered, 'I'm in among the roots of the oak tree, let me out, let me out!'

The young man cleared away the dead leaves and looked among the roots until he finally uncovered a small hollow and in it found a glass bottle. When he held the bottle up to the light, he saw something that was shaped like a frog, jumping up and down inside the bottle.

'Let me out, let me out,' it kept crying.

Suspecting no harm, the student pulled the cork off the bottle. In a flash, a spirit slipped out and began to grow, and it grew so fast that in seconds a monstrous fellow, half as big as the tree, was standing there.

In a thundering voice, he said, 'Do you know what your reward will be for letting me out?'

'No,' said the young man fearlessly, 'how could I?'

'Then I'll tell you!' cried the spirit, 'I'm going to break your neck.'

'You should have told me that before,' said the student, 'I'd have left you in the bottle. But I'll keep my head on my shoulders all the same. You'll have to consult a few more people before I let you tamper with my neck.' 'More people, indeed', said the spirit. 'You've earned your reward and you shall have it. Do you think they've kept me shut up in here all this time out of kindness? They did it to punish me. I am the mighty Mercurius, and when somebody sets me free, it's my duty to break his neck.' 'Not so fast,' said the student, 'first I've got to know that you really were in that bottle, then I'll believe that you are truly the mighty Mercurius.' 'Nothing could be simpler,' the spirit replied haughtily. Whereupon, he pulled himself in and made himself as thin and small as he had been before and crawled right through the bottle neck. No sooner was he inside, than the student shoved the cork back in place and tossed the bottle in its old place among the roots of the oak tree. The spirit had been outsmarted.

The young man started back to his father, but the spirit cried pitifully, 'Oh please let me out, please let me out.' 'No!' said the young man, 'you can't fool me twice. When I catch somebody who has threatened my life, I don't let him go so easily.'

'If you set me free,' said the spirit, 'I'll give you enough to last you as long as you live.'

'No,' said the student again, 'you'll only cheat me again.'

'You're turning your back on good fortune,' said the spirit.

'I won't hurt you, you'll be richly rewarded.'

The young man thought to himself, 'I'll take my chance, maybe he'll keep his word.' So he pulled out the cork and the spirit came out as he had the first time and stretched and spread until he was as big as a giant. He handed the student a piece of cloth very much like a poultice and said, 'This is your reward. If you put one end of it on a wound, the wound will be healed, and if you rub iron or steel with the other end, it will turn to silver.'

'I'll have to try that,' said the student. He went to a tree, gashed the bark with his axe and rubbed the gash with the cloth. The bark grew together and the wound was healed. 'It's all right,' said the man, 'Now we can part.' The spirit thanked him for setting him free, and the student thanked Mercurius for the gift and went back to his father.

'Where have you been all this time?' asked the father, 'you've forgotten all about your work. I told you you wouldn't get anything done.'

'Don't worry father, I'll catch up.'

'Catch up?' said the father indignantly, 'You don't know what you're talking about!'

'Just watch me, father, I'll have that tree felled before you know it.' He took his axe and rubbed it with the poultice and struck a powerful blow. But the iron had turned to silver and the blade had bent.

'Father, look at this wretched axe you've given me, it's all bent.'

The father was horrified, 'Now I'll have to pay for the axe, and where will I get the money?'

'Don't be angry with me,' said the son, 'I'll pay for the axe.'

'With what?' said the father, 'Can you tell me that? You may be full of book learning, but you certainly don't know anything about cutting down trees.'

Later on, they returned home together and the father said to his son, 'Go and sell that ruined axe. See what you can get for it. I'll have to earn the rest so that we can pay our neighbor.'

The son took the axe to town and brought it to a goldsmith who tested it and exclaimed, 'This axe is worth four hundred talers!' The goldsmith gave him four hundred talers right there. The student went home and said, 'Father, I have got the money. Go and ask our neighbor how much he wants for the axe.'

'I know already,' said the father, 'One taler and six groschen.'

'Look, father,' the young man said, 'I've got more money than we need.' He gave his father a hundred talers and said, 'From now on you shall live at your ease and never want for anything.' 'Good Lord!' exclaimed his father, 'How did you come by all that money?'

The student told him exactly what had happened and what a prize he had won by trusting his luck. With the rest of the money he returned to the university and continued his studies. He was able to heal all kinds of wounds with his poultice, and he became the most famous doctor in the world.

Now, can you imagine what sort of people or what cultures would dream about this tale? To begin with, the tree is, among other things, a symbol of vegetative experience, like the nervous system of the human being. Mercury would then be the wild spirit which we have bottled up in our bodies by being decent, law-abiding citizens. The father symbolizes the boy's stiffness, his teachings, his patriarchal consciousness, and the boy is the symbol of an ego which can free the spirit in the body. He is like the dreambody worker. He is you and me, who are studying dreams and body problems.

If the tale deals with a cultural problem, then we must recall that it is a Grimm's fairy tale, a tale from Europe. Europeans and Americans all have a similar dream. Our culture tells us: Be civilized, bottle up your true personality, or else let it out so quickly that you explode and go to war. Mercury is the symbol of pressure and tension, the feeling of being bottled up. He is the experience we often have of a tension headache or heart pressure, or of a stomach ache. He is a symbol of the pressured feeling everyone gets in a group which is too stiff and uptight.

Many people feel this pressure in their bodies, bottled up emotions which need to be expressed in one form or another. For example, a man came to see me with a severe stomach cramp and was anxious to have his problem solved immediately.

He came in a bit early, so I asked, 'Would you like a cup of tea first? It's so early.'

'No, I don't want a cup of tea. I want you to solve my problem.'

'I'll come back in ten minutes, then. Stay for a while,' I suggested.

He became furious with me, 'No!' he shouted. 'I want you to stay here and help me with my problems, right now.' Although I was angry with him, I realized that his cramp must have been unbearable, so I finally relented, instead of insisting on my way.

'What is it like to have a stomach cramp like yours?' I asked. For a while he was silent. 'It's like something that's trying to get out, I feel blocked,' he answered. The more I tried to work with him, the more I felt I was unable to help him because he was so totally blocked. It was like a vicious circle. He was also incredibly forceful. However, I continued with my questions until at last I heard myself saying in a high-pitched, whiney voice, 'Let me out! I can't stand it here, let me go!'

'I won't,' he replied.

'Let me out,' I insisted, 'It's too restricting in here.'

'No, absolutely not,' he said.

'Please let me go, I want to leave and have a cup of tea, I'm thirsty!' I said.

At that point, he suddenly cried out, 'Oh my God. . . .' He realized then what was happening, both inside and outside. He was silent for a while and then turned to me and said, 'This is exactly what is happening in my stomach. Now I see it. It's my feelings and needs that want to get out, and I'm not

53

letting them out.' With this insight, his stomach gradually relaxed.

The fascinating thing about this example of dreambody-work is that this man's body problems became mirrored in an outside situation. It is interesting to see how people unconsciously create their own inner problems in their environment. How they suffer in relationships with others is also how they are suffering inside themselves. This man was so impatient that he bottled up his emotions and got a stomach cramp; he was also a stomach cramp to others. Just as his gut feelings were held in by a cramp, so I was also restricted by his uptightness. His world was a reflection of his body.

A woman who had chronically recurring hepatitis, which is a liver disease, is another example of the 'Spirit in the Bottle' type. After her seventh consultation she complained of terrible liver pain. She placed her hand on her side, near the liver.

'What's it like in there?' I asked.

'It's terrible, I don't feel anything.'

'But you just told me that you have a terrible pain there!' I wondered whether I was using the wrong channel because she didn't feel anything there, or if she was just resisting me. 'If you don't feel anything there, then do you see something there?'

'Oh, yes, I can see something there, I can even draw it for you,' she said.

She made a fantastic drawing of a bag with something in it trying to escape. I pointed out what I saw and asked her if she saw what she had drawn.

'Yes, but what does it mean, what can I do about it?' she asked.

Since I didn't know what to do, I gave her a spectrum of possibilities from different channels.

'Whatever you want,' I said, 'we can play it, talk about it, fantasize more about it, listen to it, feel it, anything.'

'I want to play it,' she said. 'I want you to be the bag and I'll be whatever's inside it trying to get out.' It sounded

54

interesting, so I agreed, 'Let's do it.' She was sitting on the floor, I bent over her, put my stomach on her head and my head on her knees.

'Let's pretend I'm the bag and you're inside me.' She started to push against me, shouting, 'Let me out, let me out!'

'No, I'm a tough bag, and I won't let you out!'

'Let me out!'

'No, I won't.' This continued for a while without any definite results, so I decided to reverse the roles. Now she became the bag and told me, 'You must stay in there. You need to be in there because you have to grow.'

Again we switched roles. Crying, she started saying, 'You've put me in here long ago. I've grown far too big. I can't get out any more.'

'Oh, I'm sorry, but you have to stay in' I said as the bag.

'We can do surgery,' she said, creatively indicating the next step in her process. She took an imaginary knife and cut the wall out, she cut me, so to speak, and jumped right out of me on to the floor. She sat there for about fifteen or twenty minutes, silent and breathless.

'I feel wet behind the ears, as though I've just been born,' she said to me.

'Good, I'm glad to hear that. Who are you?' I was curious to find out.

'I'm the real woman, her deepest feelings. The deepest feelings of all.'

'What kind of feelings are you?'

'Feelings of love. I had put them away to grow, but now they want release.' She cried for a long time, until the end of our hour together. That night she dreamt that she was swimming to a brand new world and the world was full of flowers.

This is a second example of a person with locked up feelings which became somatized. In the first instance, the man's emotions were locked up in his stomach and in the woman's case they were in her liver, thus manifested as hepatitis. She couldn't allow herself to feel or express her love because she had had such a terrible life. Her mother had an addiction and she never knew her father. As a child she was frequently beaten. She learned, quite successfully, how to put her feelings in a box. Her initial process, as a child, was to repress her feelings, but now that she was an adult, and wanted to let her feelings out of the 'box', she found that she was unable to do so. Continuing to repress them became a painful process looking for realization. Instead, she had to transform her disease and learn to express those feelings.

Feelings are repressed so often and so strongly that they are forced to express themselves through a body symptom and hence cause much pain. Feelings then become violent when they are repressed for too long and may come out in dramatic diseases like cancer. Just like Mercury, locked-up emotions can become frustrated and angry and have the potential to kill!

Not only do such feelings manifest themselves in the body, but they also possess the mind, and often the patient can become suicidal because of those repressed, Mercurial feelings. I had a schizophrenic patient who had a pain in his chest. When I asked him what sort of pain it was, he jumped on my punching bag and kicked it with such force that he almost destroyed it. He was so violent and aggressive with his punching and kicking that he looked like he would kill himself in the strain. The spirit was too violent. I wondered if he had the power to control himself. In fact, like the fairy tale, this man was unable to rebottle his spirit himself, and was at the mercy of the insane asylum and pills to cork up his aggression. I helped him to bottle up his insane aggression by banging on the floor (distracting him from his punching and kicking) and insisting that he listen exactly to the way it sounded. I switched channels on him and his listening enabled him to cool off.

Let's now come back to the fairy tale of the 'Spirit in the Bottle'. The young boy who freed the spirit did so without any fear at first. But when he took the top off, the spirit tried to destroy him. The boy then used his intelligence, played a trick on the spirit, and made him return to the bottle. Spirits are never very flexible. They are predictable because they don't think creatively; they simply emote. Thus, if you keep wide awake and become flexible enough to switch channels and modes of behavior, you can sometimes be lucky enough to tame a spirit.

From the patients' stories it can be seen that it is the body feelings and the pains themselves that do the healing. If they are dealt with at the correct time and allowed to express themselves at the right moment, they will automatically heal the patient. In the woman's case, the feelings which were released from her body had had to remain there for years, and even had to create symptoms, until the time was right for her to let them out. If she had released them too early, they may have been too much of a shock for her. Her feelings told her, during the session, that they had to grow. She *had* to repress these feelings for some time. Many of the repressed feelings are infantile, such as, crying, shouting, screaming, insulting, etc., but when they have grown, as in the woman's case, they are able to express themselves more coherently.

All of us have to repress some of our inborn, mercurial spontaneity at some time. In so doing, we grow up, learn to adapt but also must pay a price by developing tension and pressure. Yet body tension is useful and meaningful. Many modern psychotherapists try to break the bottles without outwitting Mercury. These therapists encourage people to scream and kick and think that by so doing a person is healed. However, this is often a very naive attitude; if Mercury is not outwitted, as in our fairy tale, Mercury comes out, but could kill the patient. In practice, this means that by simply encouraging all tensions and stresses to leave the body, people can develop permanent physical injuries, or else they can actually go insane. One needs to be careful with tension and to appreciate it in the context of the total process. If one lets out the spirit with a bit of reserve and intelligence, without pushing and without being too naive, then feelings come out which actually heal people and help them to individuate. But if the feelings come out too quickly and chaotically, then they don't form an imagery or coherent feeling which the ego can integrate. In some cases such as I have often seen in advanced states of cancer and the terminally ill, Mercury had to be kept in so long that he began to rot the tree. But finally, near the end of life, he sometimes comes out as a beautiful and coherent spirit which enlightens the individual. The case I presented earlier about the man with the exploding stomach was just such a case.

Dreambodywork is wide-spectrum psychology, it enables you to work with dying and psychotic people. Often, with dying people, I see how the bottle's cork has been left on so long, that it becomes a matter of life and death to let him out at all costs. In such cases, the dying person sometimes goes through something resembling a psychotic episode. The dying person hallucinates wildly, changes personality and flips out completely. An inexperienced psychologist or physician might explain this aspect of dying as a psychotic episode brought about by the weakening of the physical body or by an overdose of morphine. However, an organic brain syndrome is a poor description for meeting Mercury while he is breaking free. In addition, most of these people can be brought back to this world and can integrate these wild and apparently chaotic visions. As a matter of fact, the earlier such visions and chaotic experience occur, the better off the dying person is, because in cases where Mercury is let out early, improvement in physical health often occurs. The more death experiences I see, the more I begin to believe that one of the reasons for dying, and for dying young, is to meet this impossible spirit of life, to flip out with him and bring back to this world, if you can, his immense insights and gifts. However, individuation can rarely be spoken of. It takes a master, like the young man, to outsmart Mercury. Most ordinary people either bottle him up so long that they die from him, or they let him out, can't handle the consequences and actually go psychotic. One side of the spectrum is madness, and the other is vegetative chaos, or illness. It's almost impossible to tell who is going to bottle Mercury up too long, and who will let him out too early, and who will be able to master him once he comes out in the first place.

Dreambodywork operates with the entire range of Mercury's strange doings. The therapist needs a lot of training and a lot of knowledge about body processes and mythology, usually more than is available at our medical and psychological training centers. You cannot be naive about Mercury. Breakthrough therapists are dangerous. Thank God the general public is still so conservative that they do not go in for everyone advertising Nirvana on earth or relief from tension. Tension is a crucial thing, it is the growing of Mercury, the ripening of the fruit of wholeness, and we just can't discard it too early.

This fairy tale and its relationship to bodywork shows you the archetypal patterns behind the psychological experience of pressure, tension and repression. Whoever works on these archetypal body experiences is bound to meet old man Mercury, and this figure can't be underestimated. He is nothing less than the spirit of the oak tree, the source of life, death and healing. He is a cultural problem, the wotanic, wild, barbaric spirit which was bottled up centuries ago in order to achieve our present level of civilization. Many dying people dream that their body problems are centuries old, many hallucinate near death that they were born centuries earlier.

There is no doubt in my mind that in order to live in the twentieth century, much of the ancient spirit had to be bottled up, for better or for worse. There is also no doubt in my mind that whoever meets this body spirit head on faces a tough challenge: integrating a spirit which has little popularity in the environment. Often it is easier to be sick, to suffer unbearable and unrelentless pressure, or to go mad, than it is to bring in the reality of a spirit which brings one up against social conflict, misunderstanding, and the difficulties of being an individual. You see, it is a challenge, a mythical challenge, a proprioceptive pain to be a human being.

CHAPTER 6

Dreambody in relationships

Let's now look at the relationship your dreambody has to the world around, to your conflicts, your projections, your friends and enemies. Let's see how your dreams influence your body gestures, your communications to others, and your relationship problems. But first, the term 'process' must be differentiated and primary and secondary aspects of your process introduced. Primary processes or signals are messages which you send to others, they are the ones of which you are aware. You identify your intentions with these primary signals. When I talk to someone, my primary signals consist of the content of what I am saying, the ideas and thoughts I want to convey, and my conscious intent to talk to this person.

Secondary signals, on the other hand, are all those other messages that I send, of which I am not completely aware, but which, nonetheless, influence whoever I am talking with. For example, as I talk with a friend, I'm leaning towards them, my head and eyes are focused on the flow of what I'm saying. My tone is fast and excited, and my legs and lower body are pointing toward the other person. All of these body messages describe the secondary process. In this instance, when my primary and secondary signals are in agreement, then I'm congruent. There is no confusion, I'm understood, and the situation between the two of us proceeds with ease.

However, if I don't want to be talking with my friend, if there was a problem in the background which I was unable to bring up, and which I was unconscious of, then I'd be incongruent. My body might be pointing away from the listener. My voice, while discussing an exciting and interesting topic, would be quiet and monotonous, and my legs would be twisted away from the direction in which my head was pointed. This is incongruency. I'm giving one signal with my intent, and another with my body. The two signals say: I'm talking to you, and I don't want to be talking.

Let me give you an amusing example of double signals. Once I was having trouble with one of my clients and I asked her very directly, 'Do you think that we'll ever be able to work our problems out together?' And she answered, 'Yes, of course,' while simultaneously shaking her head from side to side, obviously and unconsciously indicating 'no'. Consciously, she wants to work out her problems with me and intends to do so. But simultaneously there is a double signal of which she is barely aware and which strongly indicates that she does not believe we can nor does she want to work our problems out together.

If I follow someone's primary signals, then I could work forever and still not have worked the problem out. Primary signals turn into traps because you believe them to be the whole story and don't see the double signal which is telling you that there's more going on beneath the surface. We are all so hypnotized by the apparent meaning of what someone is saying, that we never notice how upset we become by their posture, tone of voice or hand motions. Let's say that you are sitting with someone whose shoulders are turned sideways, pointing toward you while she is talking to you. Her words are giving you a cordial, primary signal but her shoulders, which are pointing to you, are indicating somehow that she is 'giving you the cold shoulder' (as they say in English), namely, that she doesn't like you. Even though you do not know what double signals indicate, and even if you do not consciously notice them, you react to them, and this reaction disturbs the communication. You become angry without even knowing why, and you get disturbed during the conversation without realizing that her shoulder was giving you a message that she didn't like you.

The most fascinating thing about these double signals, and perhaps their most important aspect, is that they are always found in dreams. I've been repeating again and again that body symptoms are reflected in dreams, and the same is true of double signals. In fact, body symptoms are like double signals; they are dream-like, just outside awareness and not easily understood. For example, a man came to see me. He was very polite, very gentle, soft spoken and well mannered. But his arms were doing something strange. He was standing facing me with his hands on his hips, in a tough-guy stance, appearing just a bit menacing. I noticed that his arms and elbows were forming a double signal and I took a guess, 'Tell me,' I said, 'What are you dreaming about your arms? What dream did you have last night?'

He replied, 'I dreamt that my arms were being put in a yoke like a horse and that they weren't free.' This shows clearly how double signals can be seen in dreams. It also shows quite clearly that my interpretation of his signal, namely, that he had a tough guy in him, wasn't completely correct. You always have to ask what a double signal means, and not try to be a mind reader.

A woman with whom I worked recently had the habit of putting her head forward and turning her head slightly to the left so that her right ear was closest to me, giving the apearance of listening attentively. However, as I talked to her, she was constantly asking me what I said. Her speech was peppered with, 'What? what?' I finally asked her if she was having trouble hearing me, and she replied that she heard everything I said. I then asked her why she kept asking me, 'What?' She was shocked, she hadn't been aware of saying that at all. This is a total double signal: her body was sending a signal that she was totally ignorant of.

This woman has a resistance in her ears. Her intent is to be a good listener, as seen by her head and ear, yet she doesn't even hear what I'm saying. Something is not allowing her to hear. I explained this to her and she didn't understand me. I asked her, then, if she had been dreaming about ears, and she told me she had. She had dreamt about a mouse with big ears.

I suggested to her that she consciously make her ears really big. Instead of being a mouse about it, and timidly pretending to hear, why don't you get into the resistance of your ears, and refuse to listen to what I say, I asked.

'Oh, no,' she said. 'I could never do that. I'm the mother of many children, and if I didn't listen to them, they wouldn't grow up very well.' The psychology of this situation is very simple. She believed, like all of us with our peculiar beliefs, that to be a good mother one had to listen completely and attentively. Well, her ears were rebelling against this belief, and were trying to get her to do what she really wanted to do, instead of following her forced idea of motherhood. Instead of being able to be herself, her dreambody is developing a psychosomatic hearing problem as a double signal to thwart her conscious intent.

I've never come across a double signal which I couldn't place in the dream of the night before or of the past few nights. That is why double signals are so potent, one is working directly and simultaneously with all the facets of the dreambody; the dreams, illnesses, body postures and relationships.

One of the most important double signals occurs in the voice. There's a certain tone and signal in the voice. Watch carefully and notice if the tone and rhythm correspond to the content. If someone is expressing anger in a quiet, slow monotone, that's a double signal. If someone is talking about a depression with a fast, excited voice, that's a double signal, too. Watching the eyes reveals a wealth of information as well. Are they wandering around, looking up, down, to the side? Are the pupils dilated, large? Are they stinging? Itchy? Aching? The limbs also indicate a great deal. What angle do your legs make with the rest of your body? And what are your hands doing?

I strongly recommend to people interested in this kind of work that they stay away from interpreting signals. The best therapists are the ones that don't assume that they know what people are doing. When you approach double signals, you must approach them with the greatest respect, for it's the unconscious itself, and you're invading someone's privacy. The reason that people double signal is because they're at an edge, that is, they're unable to do something, they cannot allow themselves to express or do something. This makes double signals difficult to work with, and it's a touchy area for people that must be treated with consideration.

There are different ways to work with double signals, but no one way is right, each person must choose his own way. One way is to amplify them, and another way is to forbid them. Forbidding a signal has a very strong effect. By forbidding someone to make a signal, the impulse to make the posture increases. Therefore, as the need to make the posture increases, it becomes obvious to the person what that need is, and why that posture is necessary. Forbidding a signal is challenging someone to do the opposite of what they're doing, or challenging them to stop for just a moment, just long enough to get an insight into why it's so important to be sitting the way they're sitting.

Dreambodies can communicate with each other, without people being consciously aware of what is happening. Our experience of this communication is quite ordinary, we feel it almost every day without realizing it. We unconsciously pick up double signals, that is, our unconscious knowledge of human communication picks up others' dreams and processes. For example, you meet someone on the street and the talk is very pleasant and nice, yet the whole time the person's head is down, their voice is trailing off and their eyes are looking away. His words are amicable, but you begin to feel badly and uncomfortable. Without knowing why, you want to get away from this person, to avoid him. What happened specifically is that you picked up his dream, his process, which, because he is double signalling, is still unconscious to him. This phenomenon I call 'dreaming-up'. Our reactions to people are partly our own projections, our own inner dream material, and partly this phenomenon of dreaming-up, the other person's unconscious process, dreams and double signals. Most human communication is complicated by the fact that dreaming-up is present, but that no one is aware of it as such. Many relationship problems could be dealt with very quickly if we were aware of the double signals which our partners send us. It's a vicious cycle, because when our partner gives off double signals of which you are not aware, then you, too, become uncomfortable and begin double signalling.

What happens specifically is the following: Your partner is talking about shopping, while unconsciously communicating to you through double signals that he or she is depressed. You unconsciously pick up the hanging head, and slow monotone, but continue to relate to the smiling mouth and pleasant chatter about shopping. After a while, you begin to get uncomfortable, and hardly realizing it, your feet begin to jiggle nervously, yet you, too, continue the conversation. Can you imagine a scene like this? The two of you are carrying on one conversation, and your bodies are carrying on another. One conversation is about shopping, and the other is something like this: 'I'm depressed but won't admit it.' And, 'I see you're depressed, won't admit it, and I'm fed up and want to leave.'

So now you begin to see the complicated mechanics behind relationship problems. Someone begins a conversation, and for some reason, goes unconscious and is split by an edge. In this moment, the person barely realizes that he is no longer congruent, that he is dreaming and sending off double signals.

People do not realize how incongruency is self-propagating, it breeds worms, so to speak. You have a real relationship problem and simultaneously an incongruent body which is on the way to getting sick. What can you do to protect yourself against these dangers? Nothing. Relationship problems are related to unconsciousness, and since you are human and unconscious, you are bound to have relationship conflicts. But, once you find yourself in conflicts, there is something you can do. You must work at the situation. Try to find out, first of all, exactly what signal you are reacting to. Talk to your partner about this signal as if it were a double, a piece of your partner which is there and which he does not know about. Do not hold him responsible for it. Do not accuse him of creating double signals, of making dreams. Then, tell him about your dreams. If you do not have any dreams about your double signals, and if you cannot find projections of yours which have been put on your partner, then look into your partner's dreams and see if you are being dreamed-up. Sometimes you find your behavior in your dreams, sometimes in your partner's. If your partner had a dream, then you can give him some responsibility for dreaming you up, but do not forget one thing. You, too, are responsible for overreacting to something, and this responsibility can be accepted and satisfied only by working at yourself and noticing what signals you have missed in your partner and in yourself.

Jung would probably be excited by this research on double signals and dreaming up, because it's what he was working on when he discovered the anima and animus in relationships. Years ago, Jung got mixed up with relationship conflicts with his patients because he dared to sit face to face with them instead of putting them on the couch. And what Jung learned was that very often a feminine, moody-sounding comment would come out of his male patients, and a proud, male behavior would often be found in his feminine clients. He noticed that when men and women got together and fought, the man and woman would fight about one

66

thing, while the femininity, the anima of the man, and the masculinity of the woman, that is, her animus, would fight about something else.

In other words, you and your wife might be talking about taking out the garbage, but the conversation gets confused because the wife's animus turns very proud when the husband does certain things. Then he becomes very irritable and moody and tries to look hurt when the wife gets proud. His double signals are coming from the anima and hers from her animus. Can you imagine this? Two simultaneous conversations and one big mess. Naturally, you will find the anima as a female dream figure in the man's dreams, and you will also find an overly-proud, stuck-up male figure in the woman's dreams. But, you see, you cannot work on the anima and animus or your dreams only by yourself. You can always use a partner. Your partner brings out the worst of your unconscious, of your dreams, because your partner makes you aware of everything in yourself, especially those things which do not appear when you are sitting all alone. Also, you should realize that the anima and animus are only two possible interactions. Your inner mother could be talking to your partner's inner father through the telephone line of double signals, or your child can talk to your partner's stiff and nasty father, as the transactional psychologists would say. You see, dreams actually can be a big help in defining the nature of the double signal and discovering just which inner, unconscious dream figure is signalling and making trouble without your even knowing about it.

In working with childhood dreams, I've discovered that they point to a life pattern of the dreambody behavior. Very often, chronic illnesses appear in the childhood dreams. These major dreams pattern our lives, our problems with the world, and our body problems. The following example illustrates the connection between chronic illness and a childhood dream, as well as the role of double signals and dreaming-up within dreams.

A 40-year-old man with a recurring backache dreamed

when he was a child that he accidently tripped over his mother's feet, and his mother suddenly turned into a cow. The cow's head grew larger and larger until it became his whole vision. The cow's mouth was open, as if to scream, but no scream came out.

While working with this man, he first began to visualize the cow's head, the huge, distorted head with the open mouth trying to scream. I asked him if he felt the cow anywhere inside him, and he responded, 'Yes, the cow has a lot of pain, I feel it in my stomach.' I gently amplified the spot on his stomach that he pointed to, and he encouraged me to put even more pressure on his stomach. The more I pushed, the more pressure he wanted on his stomach. This was a very big man, so I really had to use all my strength. I pressed my first into his stomach and could actually feel his tense back muscles resisting my thrust. Soon, I was standing on him, with all my weight, and he was lying on the floor, very quietly and with his arms and legs spread wide. I began to feel uncomfortable, wondering how far this thing would go, not believing how much pressure this man was taking without a trace of response. I looked at him, to try to discern any double signal. Was any part of him resisting this incredible pressure and pain? No, he was absolutely congruent, lying there still. Then, I noticed something. I had stepped off of him for a minute, and he sat up. Yet, he was leaning far backwards, propping himself up with his arms. I challenged this double signal by asking him if he wanted to sit up or lie back down. He promptly answered, 'Lie back down.' I saw then that his primary intention was to give in, to lie down and avoid resisting, yet his hands were pushing him back up, to force him to resist. While I was standing on him, he never said, 'Don't do that, it hurts.' His double signalling is his inner split about resisting and defending himself. A cow is a very docile, mother-like animal. They're not very aggressive or assertive. This man has a cow-like nature. His dreambody is posing the heroic challenge to discover and develop his masculine resistance, to stop dreaming people up to either hurt him or protect him from pain. The cow in the dream opened its mouth to express pain, but couldn't. His task in life is to open his mouth and express his pain. When I was pressing against his stomach and contacting his tense back muscles, that was the first resistance I had encountered. His body symptom and his double signal were the only indications that somewhere within him he had a desire to resist, to come out with his pain.

It is fascinating for me to see again and again how illness asks for integration, how it requires consciousness by creating pain. The problem is, illness and its associated double signals always require you to do something which is exactly at the edge, at the limits of what you can do as a human being. In this man's case, his background, family and culture all insist that he be a sweet, enduring and compromising man, who does not speak up when something bothers him. Thus, his individuation process spirals around the conflict between motherly feeling and spontaneous expressions of pain. His dream stopped at the edge of his personality, at the point where he should scream, but could not. This edge splits off the reaction in him, so his body picks up the reaction instead. It sometimes seems to me as if the dreambody doesn't consider one's conscious limitations. It doesn't seem to care whether you can or cannot do something in a given moment. So it bypasses your lack of awareness and your hesitations and appears in double signals and later in symptoms, and still later in the overall pattern or myth of your life.

The less aware you are of your dreambody, or the longer you avoid making changes in your nature that your body is asking of you, the more insistent your dreambody becomes. It is a self-amplifying system and continues stubbornly until the moment comes when you get seriously ill and are forced finally to heed its message. The reversal of this pattern is a challenge to the future of your consciousness. Feel your symptoms, pick up your signals and integrate them now into your life. If you are lucky, healing may occur. If you are even luckier, you will begin to grow. Even if your chronic symptoms do not disappear, they become friendly allies ushering you into a new phase of existence in which you behave as a whole and congruent person in the midst of a rich and meaningful life. In any case, sickness can be a stroke of luck. It's a dream in the body, use it to wake up.

CHAPTER 7

The world as a dreambody

Until now, we have seen and heard how the dreambody appears in your visions, fantasies, dreams, synchronicities and even in relationship problems. Above all, we have been focusing on the dreambody in its problematical aspect as apparently pathological producer of disease symptoms, which turns out not to be a disease symptom, but a major step in your individuation. Now I want to introduce you to a paradox. Your dreambody is yours, yet it's not yours. It's a collective phenomenon, belonging to nature and the world around you. Your dreambody is you, but it's also the entire universe. This is an idea which at first inspection sounds very eastern, but instead of wandering into philosophical speculation at this point, let me tell you another story from my practice, a story which illustrates how the dreambody can also be a collective event.

The following story took place around Christmas time.* I had asked one of my analysands to visit my kids dressed up like Santa Claus, in order to play the half-good, half-evil figure of the European Santa Claus, which is still so popular

*The basic elements of this story are discussed in my article 'The Universal Dreambody' in Louise Mahdi's Open Court Edition of *Initiation and Archetype*. (To be published).

71

today in Switzerland. After Santa played his part, I took him out to a cafe near my office in order to have a psychotherapy session.

We sat in a corner at one of the restaurant's tables, and began our work. We both chattered about the evening, and after a few minutes, I noticed that I was not feeling comfortable. There was a hole in our conversation. We were talking amiably about the evening, and yet something was missing in our communication.

Instead of working with my client on the hole in our conversation, I figured I had missed a double signal and decided to focus first on myself. At once, I noticed I was a combination of processes. I was involved in the primary process of being an analyst, listening and working with my client. I was facing him and speaking with him, but underneath the table there was something else going on. A secondary process was happening in the lower half of my body. My legs were crossed and twisted away from the top part of me and from my client. I asked Santa if we could stop the conversation for a moment so that I could focus on what was happening to me. I decided to twist the top of my body in the direction of the lower half, thereby making myself congruent with my double signals under the table. As soon as I made this move, I felt better. I was no longer facing my client, and noticed that this was the way I really felt. I didn't want to listen to him. When I asked myself why, I got the immediate answer from my body that he was talking too quickly.

This answer confused me, I saw that his eyes were warm, friendly and very appealing. But simultaneously, the rapidity of his speech was agitating me. Why was he so talking so fast? I noticed that I did not want to look at him either, something was wrong with the appearance of his face.

I decided then to ask him directly why he was talking so quickly. He said that he had wanted to give me time to adjust to the cafe, but that he was in a conflict, because he really wanted to be telling me about his own problems. He was anxious to tell me that he was disturbed by his girlfriend, who was insisting that he be more related. He then wanted to tell me the following dream. In his dream, he hesitated giving a white mouse to a snake to eat. The snake spoke to him and told him to be quicker, and give him the mouse. In the second part of the dream, my client was having a conflict with a very flirty woman.

Let's take a look at the total situation. First of all, we see that Santa has an edge. He felt that he had to relate to me and couldn't go quickly ahead with the thing that really interested him and which he found personally important. This edge split up his process into two parts, one of which relates to me and the other of which is anxious to relate to his own problems.

Therefore, he sent off two signals with different messages. His primary signal was, 'Here I am with you, interested in being with you.' His secondary signal, which appeared to me in the rapidity of his speech said, 'I'm really not interested in what you're saying, and I have something else which I can't wait to get to.'

His edge and his primary and secondary signals appeared not only in his body, but in his dreams. The primary process of waiting and adapting himself to me is portrayed in his dream by not giving his snake the white mouse to eat. It's also portrayed by the anima-type, the flirty woman who has no individuality of her own, but who adapts herself to the neighborhood in order to gain the favor of those around her.

His dream and its manifestation in the double signal describe his dreambody in a nutshell. His body energy wants more attention and does not like being kept waiting. This is seen as the impatient and hungry snake in his dream. His anima, his feelings as Jung would say, is interested in the outer world. Hence, the snake is frustrated. Santa also suffers from skin rashes and nervous tension as a result of frustrating the snake.

Now what about my reactions to him? Do I simply send out double signals because he does? It's true that when he talks rapidly, I begin to turn away from him under the table. He dreams me up to be the snake in his dream which reacts to him and wishes he would get down to the point quickly. I behave like his dream – above I am related to the social situation, below I am not. But he does not 'cause' me to be incongruent. First of all, I do not know who sent out the first double signal. And secondly, I have my own dreams and body, and I don't simply react to my environment.

In fact, the night before I met with Santa, I dreamt that a Zen master had told me to come out of hiding. Let's put me under analysis now. I have a very common problem, one that bothers many therapists. I program my primary process to help other people. I don't always follow my process all the time, but try to be there for the other person. I think to myself, 'I'm getting paid by him, I really should focus on him. I should be the catalyst for him, his helper, healer and understander.' Thus, I dream about a Zen master who tells me to stop this foolish business and to be myself, to bring my real Zen self out of hiding. This means that the straightforward, unsentimental and tough personality which is in me is in hiding and must come out.

In other words, I, too, have a split similar to my client. Just as he feels he should be related to me, I feel I should be related to him. My Zen master, who appears physically in the lower part of my body, is not interested in this conventional style of relating. He's interested in the truth. When I am in a situation like analysis, in which I'm identified with the Zen master, then I take on the role of the Zen master and my client is dreamed-up by me to be the hider. When I am with someone who is more centered and stronger than I am, then I am the hider and the other is the Zen master. When I am alone, then I am aware of the tension between the two personalities in myself.

Particle and field awareness

Looking at my client and understanding his dreambody from his point of view is a very meaningful experience for him. Yet it is also important for me to understand myself and to see what my dreambody is doing in my dreams, body and environment.

However, now as I talk to you about the dreambody's communication system, I'm able, for a moment, to step outside the situation long enough to notice something. Namely, that the two of us form a unity, an inseparable system whose parts can be defined, but not divided from one another. The two of us, the therapist and client, or the two partners of any couple, form the basic particles of a system.

These particles cannot really be taken out of the system and analysed separately from the field in which they live. You cannot take a child out of its family and understand the child completely. You have to see this child within its family structure to understand it as fully as possible. When there are two people, there are three things happening. There's you, your partner and there's also the system or couple which you create and which behaves differently than the mere sum of its parts.

My client and I share a dream and an edge. Both of us dream of Zen energy or snakes, and hiding or flirting with others to win their friendship. Both of us want to be nice and adapted, yet both of us want to get down to business and follow our own process. His dream of the snake and the girl appear in my legs and my face, and my dream of the Zen master appears in his body postures.

A modern physicist would say that we have to think simultaneously in terms of both a system and its basic elements. I say that we have to think both of the individuals and of the system they create and which influences them. To know yourself, you must study yourself when you are alone and also when you are with others. You need both introverted and extroverted consciousness. You can't substitute one for the other. Knowing yourself when you are alone is not always going to help you with your relationship problems, and knowing yourself and your double signalling in relationships will not necessarily be enough to understand yourself when you are alone. You have to know yourself as a personal dreambody and also know yourself as part of the collective dreambody.

When people come together they create a couple, family, group or national dreambody. They create and are created by others. Do you remember the stories I've told you in which I was dreamed-up to be the stomach of one of my clients, or of how the back problem of a student became constellated in an automobile accident? These phenomena indicate that parts of your body get dreamed-up in the world outside you, that your partners and the world can act like parts of your body. It also means that you become one of the channels or organs for another, larger body.

When I am alone, I am both my Zen master and hider. When I am with friends, I take one side or another of this dreambody, depending upon my friends. All those people whom I gather together with are a dreambody, and each of us takes one side of it. When each of us goes home after a gathering, then each one is a little picture of this greater dreambody, characteristic of our own specific personality and imagery. This universal dreambody theory, reflected in Jung's discovery of the collective unconscious and the eastern concept of the Atman, has important implications for all human beings.

In the first place, the existence of the universal dreambody means that we are a reflection of the greater world. Our dreams are world dreams with personal imagery associated to them, and which speak especially to us. Our body problems are also problems of the world around us, we suffer in the way the whole world suffers. Our illness is a dream, it's a symptom of the incongruity of the world we live in. We can be our family's unconscious sensitivity, for example, or the world's unconscious suffering. Excuse my exaggeration, but no one is sick by himself, we all live in a field.

The existence of the dreambody means that when we are with others, they are parts of us. We are individuals, and we can act as if we are alone, but there is no direct and clear division between inner and outer. Thus, regardless of how alone we feel, we are parts of the entire world, and it influences us, just as our ability to deal with ourselves influences the world. The existence of the universal dreambody should give us a more human, more intimate relationship to both those who are near us, and to those whom we will never see.

For centuries, we have been thinking of the world as if it were centered around us. This is too personalistic, it's a type of thinking which isn't going to work in the future. It's our ability to get beyond looking at ourselves as the center of the universe, and our ability to change viewpoints so we can see ourselves as parts of a larger personality that will determine whether or not we continue world war, destructive ambitiousness and annihilation.

CHAPTER 8

Cultural change and edges

The central message of this book is that the spirit of your body, the dreambody, is a multi-channeled signaller which seeks your attention through your dreams, body symptoms and relationship problems. Moreover, the dreambody is influenced by the world around you and, paradoxically, your dreambody is also the body of the world. Healing now becomes a very comprehensive task, and the term itself can be substituted for integrating symptoms, integrating dreams and integrating the projections and problems of the world around you.

As you can well imagine, medicine of the future will not look like it does now. In probably less than half a century, the man on the street will go to his doctor with a migraine headache, or a stomach tumor and will be questioned not only about his life-style and his blood levels, but also about his relationships, his dreams and his individual experience of his body. There will be times when this future doctor will work with the entire family of a patient, there will be times when he will prescribe aspirin, and there will be times when he will tell the man to amplify his symptoms and integrate the process which happens with the dreams he had recently. There will also be other times when the doctor might say, 'My dear man, go home, and wait and see what happens. Your problems are coming from planetary disturbance, and there is no sense taking your problems personally. Wait until the city government makes certain changes. Write them your dreams now.'

Though research in psychosomatic medicine done in different parts of the world seems to indicate today that having body problems is perfectly normal, there is also an increasing body of evidence that many problems are oriented by the culture in which one lives. I remember, for example, one of my leukemia patients who dreamed that a 'bone-eater' wanted to kill him. He associated 'bone-eater' to leukemia, because he said that is exactly what leukemia does, it eats up his bones. But naturally, that is also exactly what he cannot do consciously, that is, eat 'bones'. He's so shy and inhibited that he would never bite anyone. This man's dreambody has a bone-eater process happening in his dreams and body symptoms. Why can't he integrate this process and be more of a 'biter', more aggressive and direct? In his next dream, he dreamed that he was imprisoned by a church, by inhibitions which make people sweet and nice. I wondered then if this man had lived in those parts of the world where collective and cultural traditions allowed more expressiveness, more aggression and less sweetness, whether he would be suffering from an un-integrated bone-eater process?

Naturally, with this man's process, we could turn to society and make it responsible. 'If only his environment encouraged less inhibited behavior, he wouldn't be dying of leukemia,' we could say. But, in accordance with the theory of the dreambody, we could also make *him* responsible for the collective in which he lives! The inner world and the outer world dreambodies are two-way streets, and it's impossible to place blame, for we all contribute to the body as a whole. Our dreambody is part of the entire world's dreambody, yet the world's dreambody is also found within us.

Now, if you ask me what I think the world of the future is going to look like, in spite of all my optimism, my hopes and my interests, I am forced to suspect that the world will look very much like the present one: it will be a world full of edges and full of cultural rigidness reflected in the individual dreambody and expressing itself strongly in symptoms. If there is change, then it will be that the culture in which we live will listen more closely to the sick, dying and the early death cases and we'll find out whether or not the culture is able really to support the total, human process.

Integrating the dreambody into your life, bringing your symptoms into your personality and living your dreams, is bound to take you to the edge of your own personality and bring you into conflict with the world around you. The leukemia patient, for example, will come into conflict with his immediate environment if he begins to integrate his symptoms. The world around him expects him to be a passive, loving and delicate fellow. For him to integrate dying would mean radical changes for all of us.

Remember the case earlier, of the man who was dying from cancer and was making love to a woman in his dream? This dream came after he meditated on his breathing. When he meditated, he came right up to his edge. Integrating his dream and body symptoms brought him at first to an abyss, and this frightened yet excited him. When he switched from visualization to proprioception, he stepped off into an unknown channel and had a mind-blowing experience. We can't underestimate the experience of stepping over an edge, nor can we exaggerate how utterly human and simple the edge itself seems to be. For one person, the edge is being sweet and delicate, for another it is feeling the breathing. For all of us, the edge means a change, it means leaving the known and risking the unknown.

The Greeks had a very descriptive picture of the edge we are talking about. The ancient Greeks believed that a great and terrible snake was wrapped around this little-known world of ours. The limit of consciousness was pictorialized by a huge, coiled snake that terrified everyone. Meeting this snake is a heroic task, and it is not everyone's business. It needs a lot of strength and, unfortunately, not everyone has the strength to come up to their limits and step over them. Dreams, like symptoms, happen at the very edge of what you can do. Thus, dreambodywork consciously brings you up to the edge of what you can accept. If it is the right time, and the right place, if there is sufficient courage, then it is possible to go beyond the edge of consciousness and increase the size of your world.

All symptoms try to increase your boundaries. Symptoms challenge you to increase your proprioception, they challenge you to deal with pain and to switch channels with it. Your dreams help you to open your mind to a panoramic understanding of the world, to gain a greater perspective of your individual viewpoint.

I believe that the individual of the future, like the individual today, faces the lonely task of transforming himself, with or without the agreement and understanding of those around him. He needs only to know that transforming himself means coming up against interiorized cultural edges. If this transformation is to occur, he will have to disturb the status quo of the world around him as well. The person in the midst of an individuation process must know that when his symptoms disappear, a new kind of pain is likely to arise: conflict with the history of the world, of which he has been an integral part. How he deals with this conflict is a creative task which no one can predict. But one thing is certain. Becoming an individual means stepping over cultural edges and therefore, paradoxically, also freeing the public to communicate more freely. This means the collective could integrate double signals, diseases and madnesses, which otherwise only operate in the sick, dying or insane. Can you imagine such a collective?

It is naturally very hard to imagine such a collective. The first image which comes to my mind is a case two of my students recently reported to me. These students were working together with a troubled family. Father and mother were staying together, yet father had a mistress and mother was passively tolerating life, letting father be very important. Their sitting positions, that is, the 'body' of the family system, tell us about their secondary process. They were sitting across from one another, facing each other head on, while saying (i.e. primary process-talk) that they just couldn't disturb one another. The therapists recommended that they bring the body of the collective into the foreground, and amplified the seating arrangement by changing it into the opposite situation (i.e. temporarily forbidding the signal). The seating arrangement was changed and the father sat next to mother. This situation brought out the meaning of the previous body position, because when they were next to one another, their antagonism came out. A nasty battle occurred and mother came out with her strength to father who was then forced to change. So you see, change in this small collective happened by bringing to awareness the meaning of the secondary phenomenon, the body positions of the family unit.

Cultural change

How does change work in communities, nations and families where there is no therapist to notice double signals, group body situations, territorial signals or dreams? How does change in our world happen where there is no one, except perhaps God, who stands over us and observes our behavior? Here we come up against a very important question, the understanding of which is linked with the future of our planet.

We know that change in partnership, individual or family, perhaps even in a nation, begins when people are up against an insoluble, impossible situation, for example, things like love, death, disease, bankruptcy, separations, etc. If absolute restrictions did not exist, there would be no great motivation for change. Without these restrictions, it would be easier to send a child into a mental hospital, to break up marriages, or to simply let someone die. Without the binding glue of love, or of necessity and death, change in groups rarely happens.

If a group can't break up, if they must exist for one reason or another, one of the basic components for change is available. Then you can work with this group in many ways. You can deal with the dreambody by trying to integrate its sickest or craziest member, the one who carries the unconscious process. You can work on the physical positions of the people, you can work with their double signals or their edges. There's quite a bit you can do in order to make them into a more fluid system which is self-integrating.

Theoretically it is possible for a family or group to change when the majority spontaneously changes itself in the direction of the minority. I, personally, have never witnessed such a change, though I am certain it is possible. Most changes come from some individual who is, at first, physically ill or who behaves insanely for short periods of time, but who is still basically strong enough to maintain the primary process of the group. If one member of a family chooses to bring his body experience or his fantasies into the group in such a way that the majority of the family does not feel threatened, then the whole family changes. By extrapolation, we can think the same way about our earth. We, as a group of humans, are a family living in one house. For the moment we are all stuck together here. So we are faced with a sort of insoluble situation. We can kill each other but we cannot avoid each other. The more people who live on this earth, the more desperate our situation becomes, the more it is necessary for us to learn how to get together.

Like the family of our disturbed adults and children, we, too, insist that the world is OK the way it is. The mad people and the physically ill should be put away, and we don't want to listen to them. We maintain our lives as best we can and occasionally split into world wars in which we kill one another, but we don't reflect much upon the nature of war, nor do we succeed in doing something which will change the state of things on this earth.

My guess is that given individuals will change this situation. A given individual, filled with the dreams, the body problems and the madness of the collective unconscious will, every now and then, have the strength to believe in himself. He will see through the insanity of the world he is living in, its double signals, its edges, its lack of genuineness and he will listen to his inner suffering. I suspect that such individuals in the future will be able to step up and over the edges of their private groups, take the ridicule and misunderstanding of their neighbors, weather the storms which arise when change is in the air, have patience, and hold out until the majority is ready to change their identity. If my studies of family dreambodies are correct, then I would predict that one individual who listens to the secondary process and brings it across into this world will be sufficient to change his immediate environment and the world around him, too.

CHAPTER 9

Working alone on yourself

Dreambody also lends itself to being able to work alone on yourself. It's very important to try to work alone and be independent of a therapist, because most therapists have a tendency to program you into their systems. But it's also difficult to work alone for several reasons. In the first place, working alone requires a lot of inner discipline. Without an inner, meditative discipline, it is hard to do. If you work with a good therapist, then his ability to observe increases your awareness, too, but when you are alone, your ability to open up to new and interesting signals will depend entirely upon your own curiosity. This, too, is another difficult aspect of working alone. During one of my training seminars, I once tried to calculate the number of purely somatic possible signals of which a highly trained therapist would need to be aware. I arrived in the vicinity of four hundred differentiable symptoms, signals and processes. The average student of dreambodywork needs about four years to notice at least three hundred of these and to learn how to work with them.

Working alone can also be seductively entertaining and is likely to be used to avoid the pain of facing real outer problems. However, if you are in a very lonely position in life, if you've tried to work out your problems in a realistic way on the outside, or if you are isolated from people who might help you with yourself, for instance in a hospital or a home alone, then you have no alternative than to enter, with or without assistance, the world of your body. Working on yourself may help you to stand on your own two feet, to find your own center, to re-own your body and it can be a worthwhile alternative to hearing about your inner world from some professional who may not have the right feeling towards you.

Dreambodywork alone is a research topic in itself. Until now we have the essentially introverted method of active imagination developed by Jung, which operates, more or less, with visual phenomena such as dreams, or auditory phenomena such as internal dialogue. Active imagination was Jung's term for following the visual process, or the associated internal dialogue, by writing it down and then interacting with it in your own way, bringing your own individual personality and questions to the visions and voices. Dreambodywork takes Jung's philosophy of active imagination, namely, its relationship to the process of the individual, and broadens it so that it becomes multi-channeled. Now, there's a more complete way of working kinesthetically and proprioceptively. These body channels are especially important, of course, when you are sick. If you try to visualize when you are sick or in a proprioceptive experience, then your visualization will not connect to your process and the essence of your problems will remain untouched.

Phase I self-exploration

Dreambodywork means essentially becoming aware of a signal, determining the channel it is in, and then amplifying this signal until a process begins. Thus, if you are feeling ill, then the dreambody is operating in the proprioceptive channel, and you will want to work with yourself, accurately and exactly, in this channel.

The first step is to feel your symptom. Focus intently upon feeling sick, whatever that might mean to you. For the moment, forget whatever you *think* is wrong with you, and turn your attention to your experience of the illness. Feel it and study it as if you were a scientist investigating the nature of an unknown part of the human being. To do this best, you need a beginner's mind. In this way, you can leave the known and familiar thoughts about the body and play Christopher Columbus, off to a new world.

If you have a small tremor, be exact, examine the aches and pains around the tremor as if you had never felt them before. See where the tremor originates, is it linked to your pelvis? Does it start in your back, or even outside your body? Do not be content with general terms like nausea, heart palpitations, headaches, arthritis, fever, multiple sclerosis, eczema, stomach ache, tension, etc. These are general terms. I want you to explore your symptom and be accurate, patient and as specific as possible. This exploratory stage is very important because you are leaving your medical knowledge, which explains things but does not experience them, behind. Go into the details of pressures, find out if they change, feel them, you might even paint them on your skin. Or you could take a polaroid picture of it and use it as a meditation object in the future. Go into the details of temperature problems and variations of heat and cold. Does your pain have a geometry to it? Does it radiate? While you are studying your pain, it is very useful not to move. Just lie in bed in order to be able to feel your pain better.

Phase II amplification

Most patients, when suffering from a great pain, move, in order to avoid feeling it. If you can, keep still and amplify the pain. Increase your focus on the pain of the symptom. Cramp your muscles a little more, feel your head throbbing, your skin itching. Don't scratch! Don't do anything just yet to reduce the discomfort, but instead, freeze and experience yourself. Experiencing pain like this is like dealing with a rare, never-seen-before animal, and you must watch closely and meditatively what is happening without falling into the trap of explaining or avoiding the pain. If you find it difficult to amplify the body symptom, then the chances are you haven't experienced it fully. One way to totally explore a symptom is to describe it to someone else. Tell someone exactly how they, too, can create the pain, or tell someone what it is like to be inside your body.

Phase III   channel changing

Now the foundation for your dreambody exploration has been laid, and the third stage begins by itself. If you stay with your amplification long enough, an amazing thing will happen. After a while, you'll reach the absolute limit of what you can bear, or what you are able to experience, and a channel switch occurs. This means that your experience of your aches and pains will suddenly switch out of the feeling realm and before you know what has happened, you'll be seeing, hearing or moving. Of course, it is possible that your proprioception remains constant. I've seen many cases like this, where the function of the symptom is to bring the person into awareness of the body, and simply feel themselves as a living organism. But when channel switching does occur, you'll be amazed at how subtly and quickly channels change. In fact, most people assume that they've lost focus, because one minute they're focusing on their pain, and the next, they're thinking about their neighbor, or listening to a piece of music they heard the other day. If you want, you could return to your pain, but if I were you, I'd realize that your process has switched from a proprioceptive channel to an auditory or visual experience. Your job now is to be a lightning quick and impartial observer, and stay with these changes as the dreambody changes forms.

Your task now is to amplify your dreambody process in this new channel, just as you amplified your proprioception. You can see a knife with a blade in the center of your pain, a fire in your sore throat, an iron clamp in your stomach, a rock on your backache, a drummer in your headache, a bomb in your tumor, etc. You could hear voices and conversations going on, or fights and battles or music. Or you could begin to move and want to move further. You may have some background in Jungian psychology which tells you how to deal with images, or Gestalt psychology, which helps you work with voices, or dance and yoga which help you work with movements. Again, how you amplify in the visual, auditory or kinesthetic channels depends upon the background and education you have in psychology. You may be interested in reviewing the examples of this text and assembling the methods I used in amplifying processes in various channels. The important thing for you to realize is that regardless of how you deal with your visions, voices or movements, you now have a second viewpoint, a picture, sound or motion which reflects the body symptom that you were previously just feeling. Now you know, in a different language, what your body is doing. This second channel is your dreambody's own way of trying to communicate to you its nature.

If you are like the young man in 'The Spirit in the Bottle', you will talk to the pressure, now visualized as a ghost-like spirit. The boy did very well by interacting with his dreambody aggressions, not simply letting them out, and not quite keeping them in. If you are like one of the many people who follow their dreams, you will notice that what you see, hear and do as a result of having amplified your body signals is reflected in your dreams. You may now choose to work with your body problems by examining them as your dreams, by fantasizing more into the dream, making a story out of it, associating to the images, talking to them, playing them, or whatever is right for you.

When your process has switched channels, continue to

follow what happens with the same accuracy and open-mindedness. If you are fantasizing about some scene, get into the scene and examine all the figures in your imagination. If you are hearing a voice, find out whether it is male or female, old or young, talk back to the voice, ask it questions. If your body begins to move without your willing it to, then follow the movement. Go very, very slowly and follow your movement, sit up very slowly, move your legs very little, discover how your muscles are tied up to your motions. Take your time. If you are patient, your dreambodywork will enter into life and you will simply be very aware of everything you do, see, hear and feel. This is the point. Where your dreambody will lead you is hard to tell. Perhaps to better health, perhaps into deeper feelings, or perhaps even to an inner, spontaneous insight.

Phase IV   completing the work

You will know when your work is finished. Either you will feel better, or you will have gained some insight into your symptoms and be able to associate an inner or outer conflict with your symptom. Your body problem may be a motivation to dance or to speak out or to write. In any case, the channel change gives you another channel, another way of experiencing and understanding your dreambody process.

There are some people whose process goes even one step further; from illness, to healing and still further to understanding. This last step isn't for everyone. Some people stop when they feel better. But you may want to ask yourself the following questions after your work: How does your dreambody work fit with your dreams? What meaning does it have for your life as a whole and for your individual problems specifically?

Recently, I saw a woman who came to me with a strong cold. The grippe gave her the feeling of exhaustion. Her eyes were half closed and I realized that in this introverted condition she was a good candidate for dreambodywork alone, where I was a bystander. She closed her eyes, lay on the floor with a blanket over her and focused on increasing the experience of her heart beat. She then felt like she was falling. This went into a visualization in which she was falling. Suddenly, she remembered a dream from the night before about diseased trees. She felt very light and much better, sat up after three-quarters of an hour and began to talk. She wanted to figure out how her sickness, dream and world conflicts came together.

This last phase of the work we did together. Her trees, that is, her vegetative process, was ill because she had been doing too much pushing, rushing and doing. She needed to be able to let go of ambition and fall, and become a quieter tree. In her relationship battles and her professional life, as well, she needs to be a quieter tree. If she doesn't do it consciously, she gets a cold and her body quiets her all by itself.

The great demons

You know that your dreambody work has touched the body when your interactions with your feelings, your voices, visions and movements have changed your symptoms. If you learn how to develop a disciplined, meditative focus and how to amplify and accompany the typical change of channels, your body experiences will change and stay changed as long as you are able to complete and live the implications of your dreambody fantasies.

However, I must warn you of the three demons which will try again and again to disturb your work and keep your success to a minimum. This first demon is disguised as your local apothecary. This demon looms up and tries to keep you from beginning in the first place. The temptation to alleviate your pains with aspirins and medication blocks any attempt your dreambody makes to increase your own inner awareness.

The second demon is impatience. It always tries to upset your discipline and focus by telling you that you have lost track of what you are doing. Impatience implies goal orientation, and if you're impatient to get somewhere, you're not able to go the winding route of dreambody process, which circles endlessly from one channel to another.

The third demon is your death. Naturally, death can also be an ally, but for a good many of us, death is a problem. It whispers in your ear that you are sick and dying, and tries to convince you that if the next stop on your trip isn't health, you're done for. Death tricks you into wanting only to heal yourself and will not allow you to suffer the difficult focus on pain or appreciate the fact that what you call a pathological symptom is an unknown dream pressing for realization. Death says, 'If you are not immediately healed, you have failed.'

As far as I know, there are no guided short-cuts which give you instant discipline or which avoid pain. No healing or growth program will ever fit everyone, thank God. What happens to you once you have chosen to develop discipline, focus and amplify your dreambody process, will never be predictable by anyone. Dreambodywork confronts you with your own individuality, your own wise 'dreambody guru', who will teach you whatever you need to know. If you have a courageous beginner's mind, and the attitude that you are an unexplored mystery, if you are humble, open and determined, your dreambody may teach you that biological life is also an immeasurable wonder.

CHAPTER 10

Dreambodywork verbatim

I'd like to give the reader a feeling for the details of dreambodywork in an individual session. Of course, there's no such thing as typical dreambodywork, because it depends so completely upon the individual natures of the therapist and client. Yet, it's still possible to learn from the details of a specific case. I chose to transcribe one of the tapes made at a training seminar because the work was aimed at demonstration and explanation in contrast to a private session, where process work proceeds without the expressed purpose of teaching. Moreover, the following transcription is suited to my present purposes because the seminar participant in question has an especially strong verbal-auditory function. Thus, she reported most of her feelings, visions, voices and movements, in contrast to a proprioceptive, kinesthetic or visual person who would feel a great deal, move gracefully, dance or fantasize, without the slightest interest in verbalizing these experiences.

The seminar participant wanted to work on herself because, as she said, she wanted to understand her body better and thereby gain autonomy from medical professionals who had not helped her with her somatic problems. Lee, the seminar participant, is about 35 years of age, attractive and powerful looking. She has firm muscle tone and moves very little, while speaking softly and exactly. At the time of the recording she was pregnant for the fourth time and preparing for her fourth abortion. Several months earlier she had been involved in a nearly fatal bicycle accident. She also recently suffered from what she calls a 'physical collapse', a symptom characterized by strong spasms which cramped her breathing, exhausted her and made it impossible for her to work. She already has gone through various unsuccessful medical treatments, including an occult healing session.

The following work occurred over a one-hour period of time.

Transcription of Tape	Comments
Arny: Hi Lee. Lee: Hi Arny. A: Well, what's happened to you lately? L: Well, I quit my job and uh, I went through a physical breakdown. A: A physical breakdown? What does that mean? L: Well, it means that I went to the doctor, took all sorts of tests, and they said nothing's wrong. But for two months, I couldn't do a thing. By ten in the morning, my color was red. I felt like I had mononucleosis, but I attribute it to a physical collapse. Related to my not knowing how to keep things in balance. I couldn't get up, I was	Both Arny and Lee are sitting on the floor with the others. This conversation begins spontaneously, without Lee being asked, or overtly volunteering, to work on herself. Lee's experience of a breakdown, tells us that she has spontaneous kinesthetic experiences not under her control. There is no 'I' in the sentence about her breakdown. She does not actively propriocept, or feel her body. Her main channel is seeing. Here, she describes the breakdown, not by how it felt, but by a color. Here we see that 'things get out of balance' and may suspect that she, too, needs to lose equilibrium.

very tired. My heart was beating very loudly and rapidly in the morning. I would try and get up, and just couldn't. I wanted to stay in bed, I couldn't work, but had to.

A: Did you have any internal cramping?

L: No, not at that point, that came later.

A: Later? What happened later?

L: Continual stuff, lots has happened. Well, a year before this is when I had my first cramp attack. I went to the doctor and he said nothing was wrong, I'll be OK. Recently, I had two attacks and they were pretty serious.

A: Attacks of what?

L: Well, they came on when I was jogging. They were not a stitch, and they would last approximately five days. They are higher under my rib cage and under my abdominal muscle here (shows Arny). And it's a lot of constriction that comes out and like an involuntary contraction and affects my breathing and it reminds me of labor pains, really. I'll get these sharp pains maybe every

Again, lots of motion happens to her without control. On the other hand, she has no energy to get out of bed. Thus, her kinesthetic channel will be an important part of her process.

Here the therapist may ask himself why L. is being attacked and what or how the cramp behaves.

The strength of pain is usually proportional to the lack of proprioception.
Is she pregnant?
With what?

95

five or ten minutes. The
pains continue through
the night, as I'm sleeping
and then they'll slowly
kind of diminish over a
period of about five days,
then they'll go away. If
I'm not breathing proper-
ly in a relaxed way, if I
seem to be uptight, it
could bring on a cramp.

A: How do the cramps stop?
Do they wear out?

L: Yeah.

A: By themselves, automatically?

L: Yeah, and I try to really
get in touch with them,
visualize what they look
like. And try to relax that.
Also, the reason why I
have been interested in
coming to this workshop
is that I really need to
know how to interpret
the signs or the messages
or the signals that my
body is giving me and
understand what they
mean, so I can do some-
thing to take care of my-
self without getting sick,
some real bad illness.
And if I do get an illness,
I want to know how to
take care of that myself
because I have little faith
in medical science. I was
also in a very serious bicycle accident this year.

Self-styled relaxation always tries to
annihilate the unconscious. She
wants to be relaxed in consciousness
and will not tolerate uptightness,
even though that's exactly what her
body is doing.

Pain is a proprioception. Thus,
visualization of pain switches it out
of its original channel and presses it
to be what it is not. Such visualization can therefore increase the pain,
automatically switch channels itself.

Here she projects her own medical
routines and theories such as relax-
ing, eating healthy foods, breathing
deeply, exercising, etc., on to the
medical profession.

In May. Where I could
have died. I was in the
hospital. I was riding,
well first I was on my
bicycle, I had just bought
it and I was riding with
another woman who
stopped right in front of
me and my reaction time
wasn't fast enough. I ran
into the back of her head
with my nose. And hit
her twice. Anyway, it
was an incomplete frac-
ture on one of those
deep, high bones. It cut
into a posterior artery
and they couldn't stop
the bleeding. I haemorr-
haged through three
packings before they
brought me to the hospi-
tal. And they said if they
couldn't stop the bleed-
ing they'd have to do
surgery and find out
what was bleeding. Be-
cause you can die from
those kinds of things. So I
had my first experience of
complete terror. For a few
days the only thing that
kept me alive was being
on Demerol every three
hours.

A: Wow, you had a hard
time.

L: Yeah, and that's not all
(breaks out into loud,
embarrassed laughter). I

The unconscious process appears as
an accidental process. Here, she
'runs into someone' and 'hits her
twice'. An accident can be integrated consciously by 'banging into
someone' with awareness, i.e. getting into a conflict.

Instead of staying with the process
of banging into someone, she goes
off on a medical trip and tries to
explain, instead of feeling what
happened.

just had a mammograph, but my breasts were OK. I'm concerned about breast cancer and bringing that on myself. I had one test and there were some questions, so I had a mammograph and it's OK.

A: A lump in your breasts, a hard spot, or what?

L: No, like when I've been angry or something, things come up in my head about getting breast cancer. Hell, I don't want to bring this on myself, is this an anger thing, or what's going on?
And if that isn't enough . . .

A: Uh, uh, it's not enough!

L: (Laughs loudly) It's not. Well, this doesn't even upset me interestingly enough. It should, but it doesn't, and that is, I'm pregnant for the fourth time and I'll have to get another abortion. I have no idea how I got pregnant (laughs, loud and embarrassed).

A: Zeus could have done it.

L: (Laughs) Really, I've been on natural birth control for two years, I'm very in touch with my body, I know what I'm doing (voice begins to

'Bringing cancer on myself' seems to be a modern form of confession. Today, 'thanks' to modern psychology, people feel that they sin when they get sick, instead of seeing their illness as a meaningful occurrence.

crack) I don't know how
it happened.

A: Why don't you want to
have a baby?

L: Hmm?

A: Why don't you want to
have a baby?

L: I don't know, but I keep
getting pregnant. I'm not
sure I want to be a single
parent and do that trip.
That's how I was raised
and I don't want to have
that.

A: I see.

L: I mean, if I was to do that
I'd want a healthy family
unit. I don't know if also
at my age I can do it, if I
can make the commit-
ment for sixteen
or seventeen years. So I
don't know. So that's it.
There's a lot happening
with my body and I don't
know how to read the
messages. Like the
bicycle accident, why the
hell did that happen? It's
real serious.

A: Umhum. I hear you talk
about the relationship
with your body as if you
organize your body. You
have a good program,
you *think* about what a
body needs, like, for ex-
ample, exercising or
watching your body and
trying to find out when

She doesn't hear the question at
first, and then doesn't answer it
directly. Why not? What is trying to
come to birth in her?

The real question is: Do I want to be
single and without conflicts or do I
want to be mother and part of a
family?

you're ovulating by taking your temperature and checking your cervix and all that. You have an outer relationship to your body and what I notice is that you don't have a proprioceptive experience of your body. And that's a feeling from within of what is actually happening. Communicating with it on *its* own terms.

L: That's hard for me and I wonder if that's why it goes to extremes like the bicycle accident.

A: I think it's possible. I'm not sure myself but I'd like to work with you on just that.

L: Yeah, I don't have a real intuitive sense to pick up on subtle things.

A: Well, it's not intuitive, that's why. You can't use your intuition to pick up on body signals. It's dangerous to do that, to try and be intuitive about your body.

L: I see that's what I've been doing.

A: Right now while you are sitting there I wonder if you can tell me, verbally, but not too quickly, exactly what's happening inside your body. Feel it

One could start the work anywhere. Here I pick up on her weak proprioception and use her strong auditory channel to investigate her body feeling.

and give me a description of it.

L: OK. That's easy. I think it's easy. I'll try to describe it. Around my cheeks and through the back of my head there's tingling. You know and I'm feeling the usual from my neck on down, the usual struggle to (takes a deep breath) cut off my breathing.

> Proprioceptive feelings are lumped together, undifferentiated. She feels the 'usual' because she is in an inferior channel. Her proprioception isn't used much, thus it is filled with intellectual opinion.

A: You know that very well, something trying to cut off your breathing. How did it do that? Feel your chest cavity and your upper chest cage and your rib cage and see if you can find out how you cut off your breathing.

L: Yes, it's hard for me to feel that. I keep getting into a visual place.

> This is a statement about weak proprioception. It tells me not to ask too much about feeling and to go on with images.

A: That's interesting that you visualize what's happening. Well, tell me what you visualize.

L: My vision is like a black cloud or atmosphere or vapor that closes in around my chest cavity and in my breathing area, and just very slowly, starts to consume me. Not destroying, not eating, not that kind of consumption, but kind of taking over very subtly

> She has a vision of a body feeling and a movement because she sees something capable of 'closing', 'destroying' and 'consuming'.

101

(makes a noise like the hiss of blowing wind).

A: (Arny amplifies noise of wind) How does it go? (Lee laughs) Yes, show me again.

L: (Lee starts to make the noise like the wind) Just very quietly and starts to cut it off, that's how it is right now. There's other times when it is not that quiet.

A: Quietly and slowly cuts it off.

L: Now it does, because I'm safe here. If I'm in a place where I'm not safe, I find myself holding my breath very, very quickly.

A: Yeah? How do you do that?

L: I contract my abdominal muscles.

A: Like how?

L: I just tighten them up.

A: How do you contract your abdominal muscles, like this? Uh, uh.

L: And also my rib cage muscles, all these muscles, the chest muscles, in this move-ment. I just feel myself, everything tightens up. Which isn't happening now, but . . .

A: What *is* happening now?

L: (sighs) Right now I feel a blockage in my throat.

Here, visualization switches to the auditory channel.

It is difficult to follow the logic in the content of what L. is saying. But if we follow the verbs we find that she feels safe seeing and hearing her body process and that now she may be ready to feel it directly. Her strength comes out only if threatened.

This sort of chaotic report is typical of the beginning processes in an inferior channel where many things

102

A: You feel a blockage in
your throat?
L: Yeah.
A: Strangling?
L: Yeah. It's hard to
swallow and it's like the
door closes there, it's like
the breathing passage
isn't free.
A: Uhhuh.
L: And of course, the top of
my head always gets
(giggles sadly) dizzy and
light. And then it stops
here and goes to about
here and there's no place
for all this pressure to be
released.
A: There's a lot of pressure
in there that can't be released?
L: Yeah, (she pauses, feeling head then points to
throat).
A: I see, what do you feel up
in there? (throat and
head).
L: (sighs) The tautness, constriction, hard to
swallow, it almost feels
like . . .
A: Why don't you go ahead
and feel that tightness in
your throat. Study it for
yourself. See what it's
like to have a tight throat,
until you're ready to tell
me how to make a tight
throat in myself. Study it
in the greatest detail. (it's

happen at once without control.

She's back in proprioception.

A door closes. I ask myself, how
able is she to make boundaries for
herself?

quiet as Lee studies her
tight throat)

L: (after a few minutes of
silence) I feel what hap-
pens is, what's the thing
back there, the tonsils.

A: What does it do?

L: It comes up. It kind of
comes out of the way.
And it's like the throat
starts swelling to the
point where . . . it's
smaller, . . . and maybe
half its size, . . . it thick-
ens, almost entirely
closed up . . .

> Her cheeks get red, her eyes are
> looking downward, and the tempo
> of her speaking is reduced. Her
> proprioception has become very
> strong and is about to stop her
> auditory channel from functioning.
> Her voice is reduced in volume.

A: What is the change in
your voice that happens?

> Here I am amplifying the reduction
> in her voice which is communicating
> a violent internal conflict.

L: It becomes harder for me
to speak. I can hear it
drop, it makes me
hoarse. And because of
the closing off I can feel
the pressure. (she
touches her throat) I feel
a real block and I'm
scared to release it be-
cause I wonder how long
I would cry. (breaks into
loud laugher)

> Here is an obvious double signal. It
> occurs because the *idea* of releasing
> the block is an intellectual idea, not
> her body process, which laughs at
> the idea.

A: I see.

L: There's crying in the back
of it. (pause) I had one
experience which I
wanted to share with you
briefly. The first healing
body experience I had
was about two weeks
ago. I was at a doctor's
home who had heard

about my troubles. He
asked me if he could look
at my belly. I said sure.
His hands weren't even
touching me, but he had
one hand, I guess,
around my solar plexus
and the other hand must
have been over my throat
because I could feel it
tighten when he just kept
it there. And my body
went through some
reactions, with him pull-
ing that out of me or
starting some of that re-
lease. I was breathing,
very heavily, and my
body was shaking quite a
bit, and the tears
came . . .

Her recent excursion into healing
was aimed at removing her blockage, but disregarding its function,
getting her to cry or to let out
emotions as if that were the best
healing program. Her body tightens
up in reaction to healing.

A: And now the block is
back again, now.

L: I think it's always there.
It just doesn't always
come up.

Her block comes only when she
wants to be healed or heal herself,
corresponding to her idea of what's
right for her body.

A: OK. Let's not try to take it
out, let's use it and let's
see if you can repress
your tears for a moment.

L: Yeah, (happily) I can do
that.

A: Supress your tears and if
the meaning, if the func-
tion of that swelling is to
stop your voice from
speaking, then don't talk
for a moment and see if
you can suppress your
tears and your crying.

Here I go along with the body,
which is doing the opposite of what
her consciousness thinks it ought to
be doing.

105

(Silence follows as L. holds her breathing). That's right, see if you can contract and if you can keep your sadness back.

L: (After a long pause) It's interesting to keep the sadness back with breathing. I always thought it was the other way around, if I hold my breath to keep the sadness back, that I would feel ill and create more blocks. But now my breathing block is released!

Lee looks better, apparently relieved, she's smiling.

Lee is saying that her body functions differently than the way others have told her it should function. She feels better by holding in feelings. Her block disappears.

A: Yes, go ahead and release your breathing, it's a paradox.

L: (Very quietly, after some time) I feel the top of my head. . . . it feels like I have a skull cap on.

Now the block has wandered to the top of her head, let's see why.

A: You have a tight skull cap?

L: It's tight here, it's constricting, pressure, like a tight band.

A: I'd like to feel what that's like, I wonder if you can put one on my head. I'd like to feel it myself, I don't know what a skull cap is.

Explaining and demonstrating a body feeling to someone else has the advantage of making the sufferer focus more exactly upon the proprioception than would normally be the case.

L: OK. Well, you need, first to feel like you're going to be free and let something come out your head, and

it's like, 'Oh, no, nothing
is coming out!'

A: Yes, something is coming
out.

L: And the door starts closing to the top of your
head.

A: (Now acting like L., trying to break through L.'s
hands on his head)
Open up!

L: And it starts tingling and
it won't open up right
here in this area and it
just starts tingling and
constricting, a tight band
around here. (After a
moment, she says quite
suddenly with laughter)
Sometimes I've given it to
you and not to me!

A: Yes, give it to me, I could
use it, what could I use it
for? Now, listen, you can
come on to me. Go ahead
and give it to me. I like it,
it feels good, somehow.

A: Oooh, let me see if I can
get my skull cap off. Go
ahead and put it on, I'll
try to get it off.

L: OK.

A: Hey, skullcap, get off me.

L: (As skullcap) You want it
off?

A: Well, you're sort of nice,
but you're a little tense.

L: (As skullcap, putting
pressure on me) You're
such a 'good' patient!

Here, L. has her hands on my head,
she is playing the skullcap and suddenly discovers that she can give her
inner problem, her cap or constriction, to me. Here, the therapist takes
on the patient's disease, like a
shaman.

The pressure on my head feels good
to me partly because L. should be
regulating things herself instead of
leaving everything up to me. She's
playing a 'good' patient.

I am challenging her body problem
in order to get to know more about
it.

The skull cap, her cramps, are her

107

A: Yes, I'm a very good
patient.

L: I'm your cover, I'm your
cover to protect the top of
your head.

A: What for?

L: Hmm, I'm not sure . . .

A: Do you ever blow your
top, Lee?

L: Oh, yeah, I like it.

A: You like blowing your
top?

L: Yeah.

A: But the skull cap says I
can't blow my top.

L: No, I guess you can blow
your top.

A: I can?

(A very long pause, Lee is
very quiet, then Lee puts her
hands on her stomach).

A: What do you feel down
there?

L: Blood rushing into that
area.

A: What else do you feel in
your body?

L: When I start thinking
about my body it starts
coming again.

A: Good, let's let it come. I
prefer to work with you
on it, than to keep it
away. Whatever wants to
come, let's let it come.
This is the point of what
we're doing. I want to
explain to your mind
what we're doing, OK?

advisors which tell her that she is too
passive, too 'good'.

L. blows her top, meaning that she
explodes, gets into accidents, etc.,
and needs a skull cap. Either she
represses emotion or is overtaken by
it.

Dreambodywork follows an organic,
circuitious path which approaches
central problems spirally and often
takes patience and respect to deal
with.

Now the cramp goes into her
stomach.

If one is aware of proprioception,
then one discovers that a lot goes on
in this channel, just as thoughts are
almost always running through the
internal dialogue of the auditory and
visual channels.

L: OK.

A: I'm not interested in getting rid of your symptoms, yet. I'd like to use them and like to help you get in touch with them, because you said at the beginning that's what you wanted. So I'm working with all the different things that come, showing you, in a way, how to work with them also. What's coming up right now?

L: (L. puts her hands back onto her stomach) Uhh, it's getting harder now.

(L. puts her eyes down, lies down on the floor and says that she feels pains in her gut area. I tell her to feel her pains exactly as they are, and as soon as L. tries to explain to me how they are, I tell her to continue explaining and feeling her body. During this, she acts like the pain maker, and uses her hands to press on her abdomen.)

A: You be the pain maker doing that, and I'll be Lee, OK? Can we play that game?

I lie down where she was lying, assume her body position and imitate her voice and facial expression. I also use her vocabulary.

L: Sure. It doesn't really hurt.

A: (Acting like L.) Hey, you, pain maker, you're not really hurting me, what

109

are you fooling around with my guts for? (Pause, then to Lee) Just feel free to keep doing just what you are doing, Lee, and do it long enough so you know exactly what it is you're doing to Lee.

L: OK. (She focuses intensely on her hands) Well, I can't make you pregnant. (She laughs loudly and with embarrassment.)

A: Go ahead, you can make me pregnant if you want. Hey, you just keep working on Lee. Just imagine I have curly hair and breasts.

L: I can't do that. I feel embarrassed in front of everybody.

A: What would you feel embarrassed about?

L: I feel embarrassed of what I might do to Lee. (Embarrassed laughter) I don't know.

A: Well, let's pretend that everybody's left. What would you like to do to Lee? Go ahead. Everyone's left the room, and you're going to do something embarrassing to Lee that other people shouldn't see.

L: I couldn't do that.

A: I know you couldn't. (Lee

L. is acting like the pain maker, using both hands on me, pressing and pulling my stomach.

She is in an inferior channel and I'm encouraging her and amplifying her motions verbally. She is giving off facial signals which imply surprise and wonder.
Her hands are acting on their own now. She is surprised at their autonomy. She now looks at my crotch and thinks a forbidden thought.

Her embarrassment is obviously due in part to the fact that she's in the midst of a seminar with others watching, but also to the fact that now the dreambody has appeared and that an unpredictable fact is about to surface.

110

laughs) Can you see it, can you make a vision of it?

L: Yes.

A: Yes, what do you see yourself doing to her?

L: Instead of cramping and bringing this on, the vision is that I'd be caressing myself. Making myself feel good.

A: Yes, go ahead and caress her.

L: In my vision? (laughs)

A: Are you saying that you'd be masturbating?

L: Not really masturbating, but caressing.

A: Show me how you'd be caressing her, give me an idea.

L: Well, I'd caress her breasts.

A: Yeah, go ahead, here she is.

L: (L. starts to caress Arny) Oh God, I don't believe this session!

A: I don't either! If you'd like, you can also talk to her simultaneously as you are caressing her.

L: I would probably tell her I love her. And I want to, (starts to cry) . . . to take care of her.

A: Uhum, you love her and you want to take care of her. (Now, as Lee) Yes, I need love, and I need to

Here, I change channels using her strong visual channel to regulate proprioception.

So here is the unexpected information. Much of her cramping is due to the fact that she is trying to feel and caress herself. Since this is resisted, it amplifies itself and comes out as clutching and constricting.

Lee begins to caress my chest as if I were her.

I notice her embarrassment and now use the auditory channel to give her control and to deepen her proprioception.

be taken care of.

L: (L. gasps) Then it gets harder to breathe. And then she starts cramping again.

> Her sadness about needing love can now arise, but the block reappears because being in touch with feelings for herself is not yet the whole body process.

A: (Still playing Lee) What are you doing to me now, I'm Lee and I ask you, cramp maker, why are you doing that? Don't you think I know how to take care of myself? (Lee puts hand on Arny's side, and clutches him) What are you pinching me for? (Lee sighs) (pause) Yes just keep doing that with your hands.

L: Yeah, I don't know how . . . I don't know . . .

A: Yes, use your hands, get into using your hands. That's it, beautiful. Your hands, wow. (Arny is still kind of moaning, softly growling, apparently enjoying Lee's clutching.) Ohh, this is the way of being taken care of.

L: Interesting, it's like going from that to . . .

> Unfinished sentences indicate new experiences which are not quite admitted. Here, loving is transforming into some new process.

A: Go ahead and do it for me.

L: (L. moves hands to throat) I want to show it to you.

> L. is now choking me.

A: Go ahead and show it to me. Hold on to my neck,

yes, go right ahead. I'm going to be Lee and you go ahead and choke me if you like.

L: No, I can't do that.

A: You don't have to do that.

L: I'll just pretend.

A: Yes, you just pretend to do it.

Physically she is choking while verbally she gives a double signal saying that she cannot choke. I'm playing with the ambivalence to see in which direction her process wants to go.

L: I'll pretend. I'm too strong, if I really tried, I'd choke you.

A: Are you very strong?

L: Yes.

Now instead of being the victim of a throat cramp, she experiences the dreambody itself as *her* own power.

A: How strong are you?

L: I'm not sure cause I don't really ever use my strength. (voice quivers)

A: You don't?

The change in her voice tells us that now another forbidden fact has come up: She is strong and does not use her strength.

L: Except for exercise. I don't use it aggressively.

A: You don't use your strength aggressively?

Finally, we hear that the cramp is aggression – now partially actualized.

L: No, I can't.

A: (playfully) You mustn't do that.

L: I can't do that.

A: I see.

L: I don't even think I could do it if I were attacked.

A: You wouldn't protect yourself?

L: I would really question it.

A: Me too. I like the fact that you wouldn't choke my neck, but go ahead and choke my wrist. Use your strength. Uhum, wow you're strong! My God!

Here I'm amplifying her fear of strength. L. is at one of her edges, where development, body problems and dreams take place. Who is her attacker? Is it her passivity which blocks her strength?

I use her resistance, respect it and give her another means for bringing

Go ahead and see what you can do. You never use your strength otherwise? Very strong hands, try that on this one, too. You've got good, strong arms, too.

(L. breaks into loud laughter in a definite contrast to the low monotone she previously used, as she throws herself against Arny)

A: Yeah, do it this way, strong arms! (It's quiet except for the grunts of exertion as Lee uses her strength)
L: You know how I'd like to use my strength?
A: I'd like to know.
L: I'd like to be able to tell people to fuck off, (laughs) to fuck off!
A: You'd like to say that?!
L: Yeah, I'd like to be able to stick up for myself, and use it that way.
A: I see, fuck off.
L: Yeah, leave me alone, you know, whatever. I'd like to, um . . .
A: Fuck off. You'd like to be able to say, fuck off. (L. laughs hysterically) Fuck off, something like that?
L: Yeah, I mean, maybe saying fuck off politely, maybe not quite fuck off.
A: Why don't you say fuck

out her physical strength. L. immediately picks up the suggestion and grasps my arm in a demonstration of power.

Now she becomes more congruent, her tone of her voice, her inner spasms and her outer show of strength all give one signal: strength.

Now the work is completely in the proprioceptive and kinesthetic channels. Suddenly, as the fight intensifies, L. makes a discovery and once again becomes verbal.

So now we see why loving herself was not enough. She needs to stick up for herself against others. Her strength must be born and she must verbally speak up for herself.

Another unfinished sentence.

Here is L.'s edge, her limitation. She would like to make boundaries, but off nicely to begin with?

L: (politely) Could you please leave me alone?

A: (aggressively) No!

L: (under her breath) That's too bad . . .

A: (again challenging her) You'd like to be able to say fuck off to anyone?

L: Yeah, I'd say, 'Hey, y'know, I don't like being here, this isn't good for me.' Or, 'I'm leaving, if you don't like it, tough!'

A: Yes.

L: (Her voice cracks) I want to do that.

A: You just did it.

L: Yeah (cries a little).

A: Makes you sad that you don't do that? Am I right about your sadness?

L: (crying) Yes.

A: Uhuh. Your strength constricts you instead of putting constrictions on your environment, you're awfully open.

L: Yes, too open.

A: Too open. You've got nice, strong arms. And I think one of the reasons you weight lift is to come to feel your own strength.

(I now pick up her body signal, change channels and enter into a push and pull contest with her again.

can't do it quite yet. She cannot push others away, so she is invaded.

These are the limits of what L. can do. This is where her development will proceed.

Her sadness is due to the fact that she does not use her own female strength.

115

Suddenly, she gets very
strong, then she backs off. I
challenge her again)

A: Here I come! (I push myself towards her) I'm go-
ing to invade your pro-
perty. (There's a cry from
Lee as she pushes back)
Good, OK. This time see
if you can verbalize as
you push me back.

L: (Lee starts to laugh and
then becomes weak) I
don't know if I can.   Lee's voice is weak though her

A: This is your limit. I know   physical stance against me is strong.
we're right at the limit of
what you can do and if
you can't do it, that's OK.

L: Tell me again about how
you're invading.

A: OK. I'm invading you by
not giving you any room
to be. I want you to be
nice and sweet, and I
want you to do as I tell
you to do.

L: (Pause, then softly) I   Her voice is dropping, indicating
don't want you to do   conflict with defending herself.
that. No, I'm not going to
let you do that.

A; Yes!

L: No, you can't . . . I've   Then the conflict goes internal, she
got a cramp in . . .   gets a cramp for a moment.

A: No luck, I don't want you
to be you.

L: I don't want to be in a   Lee's voice becomes strong and
struggle of pushing you.   aggressive, I pick up on this signal.

A: No way out of the struggle. (Lee laughs) Other-

116

wise, all the push ends
up inside yourself, as
cramps.

L: Yeah, boy!

(Lee pushes, gives another
demonstration of strength by

straightening her back and
flexing her arms).

L: You know what I just
thought of?

A: Hmmm?

L: When I was injured. I
was in the hospital. One
of my friends said to me
that he could have asked
for anything, and I would
have given it to him. If he
asked me to sign over the
lease to my house, I
probably would have
given it to him.

A: Yes.

L: And I just had a flash,
that he's right.

A: Yup, that's the flash?

L: Yeah, I'd rather just give
away my house,
than . . . (voice quivers)
say, 'No! You fucking
can't have my house!'

L: (A long silence, Lee is
quiet) I'd like to go ahead
and work more,
continue.

A: Uhum. OK. Now see
what is happening. Your
face is looking at me, but
your body is leaning back
like mine and your torso

The defence went internal, she got a
cramp for a moment, and then was
able to bring it out in a physical way
by pushing against the invader
much more strongly.

Suddenly, the channels switch, here
at her limits, she makes a discovery
and sits back.

Her sudden thought is like a dream,
giving her a picture of the problem,
the edge she is standing at.

117

is twisted, facing away
from me. That says to
me, that, for the moment,
your body is not into do-
ing what you just said
you'd like to do.

L: OK. I should watch what
my body does and not
just say things.

She looks relieved, relaxes, nodding
her head, she sits back. Now she got
the point.

After the work, we took a break and came back to discuss
the session. During the break, Lee volunteered a dream that
she recently had. In the dream Lee was staying at a friend's
house, a woman whom Lee described as 'an extremely
passive person, who can't stand up for herself at all'. In the
dream, the two of them were sleeping in a big, double bed
and the woman kept rolling over on top of Lee, and Lee
pushed her off. This dream confirmed the process work. In
the work, we got to Lee's edge, and thus, automatically
worked on her dream.

In Lee's case, the inferior channel was kinesthesia. Here
she is at the will of the unconscious. The inferior channel is
experienced fearfully, autonomously, as something out of
control. For example, in her dream, her friend rolls on top of
her. She experiences 'physical collapses', and was 'thrown
forward' in an accident. The ego does not function as an
active director, but as an experiencer and reactor. 'Collapse'
and 'throw' are kinesthetic verbs, words of movement. If
hearing was an inferior channel, she would hear voices. If
proprioception was weak, strange sensations would disturb
her. If visualization was weak, she would be overcome by
dreams or visions. Body motions, as well as verbs, tell us of
the inferior channel. Weak hearing is often indicated by
putting the left or right ear forward; weak seeing by holding
the eyes closed; weak proprioception by chronic pain. Weak

kinesthesia is implied, as in Lee's case, by her softly spoken, unmoved and unmoving behavior.

The edge of the weak channel occurs when one says, 'I can't.' This statement implies what one could do or will soon be able to do. If Lee says, 'I can't push people away', then her dream would be moving things away from herself, making room, defining herself and creating space in her relationships.

Process-oriented dreambodywork determines the inferior channel's edge and therefore, does dreamwork without even having heard the dream. In Lee's case, we worked on her pushing without knowing the dream. Processes revolve around the edge of the personality, the edge of the dreams. I often ask my clients about their dreams if they do not spontaneously tell them to me in order to check my work, to be sure that I am, indeed, following their process. Dreams apparently pictorialize the patterns of processes which are trying to happen. They are factors of coherence in dreambodywork.

You can see from this work how Lee's dreambody manifests itself physically. It clutches her real body from within, it cuts off her breathing by cramping her chest when she is too soft, it twists her abdomen with spasms and chokes her throat, demonstrating its power and existence. It pushes her forward into accidents when she wants to remain withdrawn. In her conscious mind she programs herself to be a routine person, a passive, soft woman who issues monotonous, unaggressive verbal signals. Thus, her real body is like the rest of our bodies: an incongruent outline which only secondarily expresses its dreams. It acts like a mechanical apparatus which is vitalized but also deeply troubled by an unknown spirit.

For Lee, individuation means congruence with her dreambody. She must live her cramping, be more forceful, active and definite. Congruence requires the courage to step over the edge which she has defined for herself in relationships and to challenge the foundations of her consciousness. It implies first feeling symptoms as they occur proprioceptively, and then letting them express themselves, and particularly in Lee's case not to assume or theorize their meaning beforehand.

The more one increases mental and physical boundaries, the less dramatic the impact between the dreambody and reality becomes. In those areas where one is already free of edges and spontaneous, one lives the dreambody almost without realizing it. However, the human condition is normally full of the simplest edges, the most elementary things which one simply cannot do. These limitations go along with unconsciousness, body symptoms, dreams and relationship problems. From the viewpoint of the dreambody, the more problems one has, the greater the motivation for individuation.

CHAPTER 11

The edge of death

Dreambody awareness increases most dramatically near death. The threat of losing our real bodies challenges the dreambody spirit to express itself more forcefully than ever. Many fears of death are based upon an unconsciousness of the dreambody which people never consider until they are forced to do so. Thus, dying people are troubled about what will happen to them at the point of death. Anxiety overcomes most of them. They panic because their whole life they've identified solely with their real bodies and have never experienced the illness and spirit which is their dreambody. This reminds me of the Grimm's Fairy Tale in which Death comes to the hero. The hero asks Death why he has come so suddenly, and Death becomes angry and says, 'You fool! I came every night when you went to sleep, and every time you got sick. I've always been around, you just have never noticed me before.'

My research with the dying has uncovered an important and informative phenomenon occurring at the edge of death. Right before death, dying people often feel that they have recovered and feel well again. They try to leave their beds, leave the hospital and want to go downtown. Some dream and later believe that they are healthy. One woman said to

121

me the day before she died that she felt so well that she wanted to leave the hospital and go shopping to buy a new dress. A man told me shortly before he died that he wanted to go skiing that coming winter because he loved powder skiing so much. Another man told me that dying is strange because you try to get out of bed to tie your shoes, but the laces fall asunder into atoms. When these dying people attempt to follow their inner feelings and visions, they naturally collapse on the floor.

Apparently, seeing, hearing and feeling continue to function in the dying person. In fact they continue to experience a body proprioceptively, though their body is only loosely attached to the real body. In contrast to a normal, healthy person, whose dreambody creates myoclonic spasms, pains and life impulses which can be associated to a real piece of machinery, the dying person's inner feelings, spasms and movements continue but are no longer attached to a piece of real machinery. Near death, dying people experience their dreambodies as clairvoyant or lucid dreamers. They feel that they can go places and often really see, hear and feel what is going on in a distant place even though their real bodies still lie in bed. Their dreambody is almost free to do the impossible because their proprioception no longer relates to the pressures, pains and agonies of their physical body.

We identify ourselves during the greater part of life with our real body, which is disturbed by the dreambody. It pierces us with pain, creates unbelievable dreams, makes us hallucinate and hear voices and it appears in projections, relationship problems and in parapsychological phenomena which spook us like a dream. Near death, however, we still think we are in a real body, but now we are the dreambody. Now, instead of being unconscious about dreams in the body, the dying become unconscious of the real body attached to the dreambody! The dying person trying to get out of bed is in the dreambody and does not realize that the real body is no longer capable of doing what he feels like doing. He wants to continue to plan for the future, go powder skiing or leave the hospital room, and is shocked to discover that he cannot do so. His new form of unconsciousness is the real world, not the dream world.

If we stand outside this process and look in from without, then we are tempted to conclude that the dreambody transcends the real body. The way we see, feel and hear during life seems to be the transcendental thing, the eternal body. Apparently, perception and channels are eternal, not the apparatus to which it's attached. My ability to move my hand while writing, my ability to see while reading, my feeling of the hot sun on my back and my ability to hear the sea behind me as it strikes the shore, are abilities which belong to my dreambody. During my life these abilities are developed by having a real body with eyes, ears and hands. But the real body is only a playpen for the dreambody. The real body limits us, but also helps us learn to walk. And one day in the future, when we are ready to walk alone, we will step out of our playpen, out of our real body. In death we move and see without our legs or eyes. We discard the real body as if it were a crutch, and we are born to perception in dying, so to speak.

But death is not just a cosmic experience of perception. A lot of it is just plain misery and exhaustion. Without awareness of your ability to perceive, that is, without the awareness that you are a dreambody, you remain unconscious of your total personality and become as confused in death as you were in life. Without the consciousness of your total personality, you think that you are either a real body, or then near death, a dreambody, instead of realizing that you are basically pure awareness which sometimes and for short periods of time can identify with a real body. Without this realization, the dying process is like a shipwreck without a life raft. Many people experience it as a flood which robs them of what they believed to be solid land. People become frightened at death, they think they are going psychotic, they fear being drowned in parapsychological hallucinations and out of the body experiences which happen near the end.

I have worked with people who realize during life that they are real people being moved by a spirit. They become aware in dying that they are spirits coming and going from a real body. Such dying people developed their ability to feel dreambodies during life. They were able to leave their real settings when they felt the call of the dreambody and went wherever it took them outside the expectations and opinions of the environment. In death, too, they stayed with their dreambody, realizing that part of them was still here on earth. Thus they came and went from this consensus reality as they needed to, and didn't suffer needlessly from severe dissociation.

Dreambodywork consists in following the dream in the body during life and following reality as it impinges upon the dreambody in death. Interesting hypotheses come from the evidence that the dreambody is basically a perception system and that consciousness means awareness of our ability to perceive. Does consciousness then mean that we remain in touch with this world in death? Do the stories of immortality mean that our greatest teachers are still with us? Is heaven freedom on earth? Why do we rush through life? Are we dead now? The dreambody may well incarnate in matter during life and become a dream near death. Do we choose the human form in order to develop our ability to perceive and to know that we perceive? The limits of our human abilities awaken us to the dreambody. The thing which you cannot bear to look at . . . that is the secret of the dreambody. The sound you can almost not tolerate, think of it, here is where the dreambody begins. The limit of your physical endurance and strength, the physical act you cannot bear, here you find the dream-body awareness. The dreambody uses our edges, but shows little respect for our limits. It creates pain and joy to announce itself, and forces its awareness on us.

If you sit on a chartered airplane flight, lack of space makes you aware of how much room your dreambody needs, and how much you normally give it. If you are pressed by time, you realize that your dreambody is not concerned with collective time. If you feel pressured while others are relaxed, you realize that your dreambody has an urgent, very human task which cannot wait. If others limit you, or internal dialogue and opinion oppresses you, then you realize that you have a dreambody and that it was born to be free. It belongs to the family of truth and not to culture or history. Just as the sea needs the land to know itself, so the real, living person needs the dreambody to retain perspective. The person should know that impossible events are especially useful. They press you to broaden limits and increase your flexibility, and make you realize that liberation means discovering the dreambody which restlessly struggles with the edges of reality. The greatest freedom from the pain of the clash between the dreambody and the real world, occurs through the awareness evoked by pain and not through the battle against this pain.

If we could step out of the life-death cycle for a moment, be fair and just observers of existence, we might be able to see the eternal dreambody as a perception system. During a greater part of life, dreams and body problems form our unconsciousness. But near death the real world becomes our dream. Thus, we can speculate that the events of this world are the dreams of the dying. Thus, being conscious at any moment means considering any remarkable perception to be our dream, whether fantasy, a body problem or a limitation in the 'real world'. Every signal is part of our personality. Powerful and disturbing information forces us to be aware that we are a dreambody. This means that we must realize that we have bodies, yet can also leave them. It means that if we have developed some form of awareness, that it may be independent of the living body. It means that near death and afterwards we have to be careful not to become unconscious of the problems and events of this world. My theories minimize death but create order where there was nonsense and chaos. Process-oriented dreambodywork with the dying usually provokes very strong, positive feedback from the suffering person.

There can be little doubt that lack of dreambody awareness is one of the causes of a lot of senseless pain and confusion near death. For example, I remember a dream which a dying man told me, a typical dream which I have heard many times. This man dreamed that he came to his own funeral, but was unhappy because everyone focused on his coffin and didn't see or hear him standing amidst the mourners. Let's look at this dream more closely. There he is, coming to his funeral, looking at his dead body and the mourners. The dead body is his present experience of the life force leaving his body. He himself is in the dreambody, which has left its connection to this real, living machine. The mourners would be a part of him which is mourning death, seeing it at the end, and thinking, 'This is it, no more connection with him.' The mourners would be a collective, incorrect idea of his that he will be finished in death, that he exists only as a real body. In the dream, he is split. He's a dreambody, but he is also sad because he does not yet know this, he still sees himself as the real body plagued by disease, and is insensitive to the fact that he is a dreambody. Some weeks later, and just minutes before his death, this man said in a broken voice that the mistake which he had made until now was thinking that he should cure his illness, instead of realizing that it wanted him to make a radical change in his life, one that he was now willing to make. 'From now on,' he vowed, 'I'm going to be an individual.'

His realization was so simple, I wonder why he had to wait until death to discover that we are all individuals. Perhaps death is the last edge, the one at which we truly begin to live as we are.

Index

121–6; experiences, 58; in fairy
tales, 121; fear of, 16, 121;
integration of, 22; of mother, 17;
phobia, 20; processes, 21–2, 24, 25,
121–6
Demerol, 97
Depression, 25, 31, 63
Diamond body, 45
Disease, 33, 126; chronic, 13; as
meaningful, 1, 5, 6, 10, 98; process
of, 47; as self-healing, 15; tao of,
10; transformation of, 56
Diseases: bronchitis, 46; cancer, 6–8,
17, 18, 20–3, 29–31, 33–6, 56, 58,
98; eczema, 6; grippe, 90, 91;
hepatitis, 54, 55; leukemia, 79, 80;
mononucleosis, 94; multiple
sclerosis, 13–15; neuritis, 39, 40;
tumors, 6–8, 11, 12, 15, 17, 18, 20,
29, 30, 31, 33–6
Dizziness, 103
'Double,' 21, 22, 40, 41, 66
Double signals, 24, 61–9, 72–4, 76,
82, 83, 84, 104, 113
Dramatizing, 35, 36
Drawing, 54
Dream symbols, 45; amplification of,
39; see also Symbols for specific
imagery
Dream therapy, 2
Dreambody, 9, 41, 45, 47, 119;
appearances of, 48, 71, 110, 124;
and channels, 45; and childhood
dreams, 67–70; as communication
system, 75–7; and death, 11, 12,
121–6; definition of, 8, 39, 124; as
diamond body, 45; discovery of, 8;
as dream and body, 8; and edges,
124, 125; as eternal, 125, 126; in
environment, 43, 45, 54, 71;
experience of, 113; in fairy tales,
48–59; integration of, 80, 83; as
multi-channeled signaller, 78; as
own solution, 15; as physical

manifestation, 119; and
psychosomatic problems, 63; in
relationships, 60–70; as self-
amplifying system, 69; as
symmetrical, 45; theory of, 79;
working alone with, 85–92; and
world field, 71–7, 78–84
Dreambodywork, 3, 4, 9, 37, 38, 41,
42, 54, 58, 59, 86, 108, 119, 124,
125; and death, 124–6; and edges,
81, 124; students of, 85; verbatim,
93–120; and yoga, 42
Dreaming-up, 65–7, 74, 76
Dreams, 1, 20, 21, 24, 25, 35, 39, 41,
43, 44, 48, 62, 64, 65, 67, 68, 73, 74,
81, 82, 89, 90, 91, 118, 126;
childhood, 67–70; of disease, 8;
and double signals, 62, 68, 73; and
dying, 125, 126; and edges, 113,
119, 120; as fairy tale, 52; and field
theory, 71–7; as information, 9; as
link to body symptoms, 2, 3, 5, 7,
8, 62, 76, 77, 89; meditation of, 35;
as mirrored in physical gestures,
3; mirroring body experiences, 3,
8, 29; mirroring disease, 3, 8;
mirroring relationship problems,
3; and process work, 118–20;
projections in, 29
Dreamwork, 2, 3, 25, 39, 42, 89, 119
Dying, 6, 11, 12, 20, 22, 23, 24, 33,
34, 58, 80, 97, 121–6

Ears, 62, 63
Eastern philosophy, 6
Eczema, 6
Edges, 64, 65, 69, 73, 75, 113, 114,
116, 118, 119, 120; in channels,
37–47; and cultural change, 78–84;
and death, 121–6
Ego, 52, 58, 69, 118
Enemies, 29
Eternal self, 21
Exhaustion, 90, 91, 94

114, 118; experiences, 94, 95;
types, 35; verbs, 118

Language, 11, 27
Laughter, 97, 98, 102, 104, 106, 110,
114, 116
Leukemia, 79, 80
Limits, 69, 116; in channels, 38, 45;
of consciousness, 80, 81; and
death, 124
Liver, 54, 55; disease, 54, 55
Love, 14, 15, 33, 55, 111, 112, 114

Magic, 29
Mammograph, 98
Masculinity, 68
Masturbation, 45, 111
Maternal instinct, 20
Medicine, 2, 5, 6, 91; men, 29; as
symptoms, 15, 18
Meditation, 35, 80, 87
Mediumistic, 41
Menstruation, 20
Mercurial: feelings, 56; spontaneity,
57
Mercury, 52, 53, 56–9; as bottled-up
spirit, 52–9
Metastases, 17
Milk, 18, 19, 20
Mononucleosis, 94
Mother, 33, 68, 99; complex, 31;
death of, 17, 18; inner, 17, 18, 67
Motherhood, 63
Mothering, 20, 68, 69
Mouse, 73
Mouth, 68, 69
Movement, 35, 37, 38, 47, 48; and
pain, 87, 88; see also Kinesthesia
and Kinesthetic channel
Multi-channeled, 45, 78, 86;
personality, 39
Multiple Sclerosis, 13, 14
Muscles, 102

Myth: and dreambody, 69; as
personal, 47
Mythology, 59

Neck: problems, 31; stiff, 6
Nervous: system, 52; tension, 43, 73
Neuritis, 39, 40
Nightmares, 21
Nirvana, 59
Noises, 7, 34, 102

Out-of-body experiences, 124

Pain, 5, 33, 34, 37, 41, 48, 54, 56, 109;
amplification of, 6, 39, 40; and
dying, 6, 7, 123, 126; and edges,
38, 69, 124; exploration of, 87, 88,
91; expression of, 69; as healing,
57; integration of, 32, 39; as own
medicine, 8; reactions to, 6; relief
of, 7, 10; visualization of, 39, 96;
working with, 87, 88, 91
Paralysis, 39
Parapsychological phenomena, 47,
122, 123
Particle awareness, 75–7
Penis, 35
Personal dreambody, 75
Personal myth, 47
Personality, 39
Phobia, 20
Physical collapse, 94, 118
Physics, 3, 75
Pills, 24, 56
Postural signals, 25, 26, 27, 60, 61,
63, 64, 72, 117
Pranayama, 44
Pregnancy, 94, 98, 99, 110
Pressure, 43, 52, 53, 57, 59, 68, 103,
104, 106, 107
Primary process, 68, 72–4, 82;
definition of, 10, 11, 60, 61
Primary signals, 60, 61, 68, 73
Process, 32; around the edge, 119;

definition of, 10, 11; and content,
10; differentiation of, 60; of
disease, 47; following the, 37; as
movement, 11; primary, 10, 11, 60,
61, 68, 72–4, 82; secondary, 10, 11,
17, 60, 61, 72, 82, 84, 119; as tao, 26
Process-oriented psychology, 2
Process-oriented psychologist, 9
Process work, 2, 10, 11, 32, 118; as
natural science, 9
Projections, 19, 28, 32, 33, 34, 95, 96,
122, 125; father, 29–31; and illness,
28–36; negative, 29, 30, 31, 32, 33;
positive, 28, 33; as psychosomatic
phenomena, 36
Proprioception, 7, 8, 33, 36, 38, 44,
45, 46, 47, 94, 95, 96, 100, 101, 102,
103, 104, 106, 108; amplification of,
46–7; and dying, 122, 123
Proprioceptive: awareness, 35;
channel, 8, 13, 37, 38, 40, 45, 46,
47, 80, 86, 96, 100–3, 108, 111, 114,
118
Psychiatry, 2
Psychology, 2, 3, 16
Psychosomatic: hearing problem, 63;
medicine, 79; phenomena, 36;
studies, 32
Psychotic, 58, 123; episodes, 58;
people, 2, 3

Rashes, 73
Reichian therapy, 5
Relationships, 19, 33, 34, 35, 54, 118,
119; to body, 33; difficulties in, 2,
3, 41, 42, 65, 122; and dreambody,
60–70, 71–7; and edges, 73, 120
Religious experience, 44, 45
Repression, 56, 57, 59
Resistance, 68, 69; to therapy, 16,
18–20
Rib cage, 101, 102
Role reversal, 55

Santa Claus, 71, 72
Schizophrenia, 23, 56
Secondary process, 17, 72, 82, 84,
119; definition of, 10, 11, 60, 61
Secondary signals, 60, 61, 73, 82
Seeing, see Visual channel and
Visualization
Self, 21
Shaking, 13, 14, 30
Shamans, 29, 107
Shoulders, 34, 35, 61, 62
Shouting, 7, 57
Shyness, 33, 38, 41, 79
Sexuality, 46
Signals, 69, 100; body, 27, 100, 115;
facial, 3, 109, 110; forbidding, 64,
82; picking up, 115, 116; postural,
25, 26, 27, 60, 61, 63, 64, 72, 82,
117; primary, 60, 61, 68, 73;
secondary, 60, 61, 73, 82;
territorial, 82; verbal, 119; in voice,
63
Skin rash, 73
Snakes, 9, 73, 74, 80
Social conflict, 59
Somatic consciousness, 36
Somatized: feelings, 55; problems, 7
South America, 29
Spinal Column, 20
Spine, 37, 39
Spirit: of dreambody, 121; Mercury,
52, 53, 56, 57–9; 'The Spirit in the
Bottle', 48–59, 89; as violent, 56
Spiritual experience, 44
States, 11, 32
Stomach, 58, 68, 69, 108, 109; cancer,
6–8; cramps, 46, 53, 54; emotions
in, 55; problems, 31; tumor, 6–8,
15
Stomachache, 52
Strength, 113–16
Suicide, 23, 24, 26, 56
Surgery, 55
Symbols: of bomb, 8; of cats, 41, 42;